How to Use This Book

KEY TO SYMBOLS

✚ Map reference to the accompanying fold-out map

✉ Address

☎ Telephone number

🕐 Opening/closing times

🍴 Restaurant or café

🚆 Nearest rail station

🚌 Nearest bus route

⛴ Nearest riverboat or ferry stop

♿ Facilities for visitors with disabilities

❓ Other practical information

▷ Further information

ℹ Tourist information

✋ Admission charges: Expensive (over €6), Moderate (€3–€6), and Inexpensive (under €3)

★ Major Sight   ★ Minor Sight

👣 Walks   🚌 Excursions

🛍 Shops

🎵 Entertainment and Nightlife

🍴 Restaurants

This guide is divided into four sections

• Essential Venice: An introduction to the city and tips on making the most of your stay.

• Venice by Area: We've broken the city into five areas, and recommended the best sights, shops, entertainment venues, nightlife and restaurants in each one. Suggested walks help you to explore on foot.

• Where to Stay: The best hotels, whether you're looking for luxury, budget or something in between.

• Need to Know: The info you need to make your trip run smoothly, including getting about by public transport, weather tips, emergency phone numbers and useful websites.

Navigation In the Venice by Area chapter, we've given each area its own tint, which is also used on the locator maps throughout the book and the map on the inside front cover.

Maps The fold-out map accompanying this book is a comprehensive street plan of Venice. The grid on this fold-out map is the same as the grid on the locator maps within the book. We've given grid references within the book for each sight and listing.

Contents

CONTENTS

Introducing Venice

Venice has been seducing visitors for centuries, its impossible watery setting and fairy-tale appearance casting a spell whose potency remains undiminished by floods, mass tourism and the many other travails of the modern world.

The city sits at the heart of a lagoon, its many islands, alleys and canals divided into six districts, or *sestieri*, three to the west of the Grand Canal (San Polo, Dorsoduro and Santa Croce) and three to the east (San Marco, Castello and Cannaregio). Each has its own unmissable sights and each has a labyrinth of timeless alleys and streets—a delight to wander for their own sake.

This labyrinth may look intimidating, but the city is easier to navigate than its looks: distances are short, a few key streets wend through the maze, and the Rialto, Venice's old commercial heart, and the Piazza San Marco, its most famous square, provide central points of reference. On your first morning, though, resist the temptation to dash for the major sights. Start instead with a cappuccino in a sleepy square, or something where the crowds don't turn you away from the city at the first acquaintance.

Then you can move to the bigger draws and finally grapple with what to see among Venice's plethora of wonderful churches, palaces and museums. Don't forget the cafés, walks, tiny shops and essential boat trips along the Grand Canal or perhaps out to the islands of the lagoon.

But in seeing the sights, don't fall into the trap of believing Venice is a sort of medieval theme park, a dead city sustained for the benefit of visitors. The population may be falling but this is still a living place; a magnificent retreat where people live and work. Visitors come and go but the world's most beautiful city will prevail for many centuries to come. For what would the world be without Venice?

Facts + Figures

- It is estimated that there are 3,000 alleys in Venice. Laid end to end they would stretch for 192km (120 miles)
- Venice has around 400 bridges
- The city has some 450 souvenir shops. Fifty per cent of the workforce is involved in tourism

SPECIAL TICKETS

A single 'Museum Pass' costs €18 and gives entry to major museums including Palazzo Ducale. There is a 'Museums of San Marco' (and other specified museums) pass costing €12. Most of the city's churches charge a small fee of around €2.50; a 3-day 'Chorus Pass' costs €8 and admits you to 16 specified churches
☎ 041 275 0462; www.chorusvenezia.org

ACQUA ALTA

Visit Venice between November and April and you run the risk of encountering *acqua alta* or 'high water', when winter weather, winds and high tides combine to submerge large areas. Raised wooden walkways, *passarelle*, are laid out on key routes to help people get around and packing some waterproof footwear is a good idea.

BEST MOMENTS

These are often away from the main sights. So take a boat along the Grand Canal just for the ride, or see the Rialto markets at the crack of dawn before the crowds arrive. Little beats an aerial view, preferably from the top of San Giorgio Maggiore, and no city offers more to those who wander at random. A trip to the islands off-season can be magical.

A Short Stay in Venice

DAY 1

Morning Walk to the Rialto Bridge and explore the **Rialto markets** (▷ 74, 77). Visit **Santa Maria Gloriosa dei Frari** (▷ 70–71), seeing **San Polo** (▷ 75) and **San Giacomo dell'Orio** (▷ 75) en route. Then visit the **Scuola Grande di San Rocco** (▷ 72–73).

Mid-morning Have coffee in Campo Santa Margherita. Visit the **Scuola Grande dei Carmini** (▷ 90) and **San Sebastiano** (▷ 88). Walk toward the **Gallerie dell'Accademia** (▷ 86–87) via San Barnaba.

Lunch Have lunch in San Polo or Dorsoduro. **Dona Onesta** (▷ 96), **Antica Montin** (▷ 96), Agli Alboretti or a snack from a café in **Campo Santa Margherita** (▷ 91) are good options.

Afternoon Visit the **Gallerie dell'Accademia** (▷ 86–87) and then explore the streets of Dorsoduro and the church of **Santa Maria della Salute** (▷ 89). If you like modern art, visit the **Collezione Peggy Guggenheim** (▷ 85). Walk across the Accademia bridge to see **Campo Santo Stefano** (also known as Campo Francesco Morosini, ▷ 33) and its church. This is a very pleasant square in which to have a break for a coffee, ice cream or an early-evening drink.

Dinner For a good option choose a restaurant in the Castello, San Marco or Cannaregio districts. Try **Alla Rivetta** (▷ 63) for a budget choice or **Antico Martini** (▷ 41) for a classy, pricey preshow meal.

Evening Be sure just to walk for its own sake or ride a boat (▷ 118) down the **Grand Canal** (▷ 68–69). Or catch a Vivaldi or other concert in **Teatro La Fenice** (▷ 35, 40), the **Teatro Malibran** (▷ 62) or one of the city's churches.

DAY 2

Morning Get to **Piazza San Marco** (▷ 30–31) as early as possible to beat the worst of the crowds. See the **Basilica** (▷ 24–25) then join the line for the **Campanile** (▷ 31). Carry on from here to visit the **Palazzo Ducale** (▷ 28–29).

Mid-morning Take coffee in Piazza San Marco, say at **Caffè Florian** (▷ 41), but be warned: it will be expensive. Then visit the underrated **Museo Civico Correr** (▷ 26–27).

Lunch Stop in one of the restaurants north of Piazza San Marco such as **Osteria Oliva Nera** (▷ 64) or **Da Remigio** (▷ 64). Alternatively, buy a snack in one of the cafés on **Campo Santa Maria Formosa** (▷ 32).

Afternoon Visit **Santa Maria Formosa** (▷ 32). After about 3.30, the churches of **San Zaccaria** (▷ 50–51), San Giorgio dei Greci and **San Giovannni in Bragora** (▷ 49) should be open. If not, the area is a delight to explore. Visit the **Scuola di San Giorgio degli Schiavoni** (▷ 54–55) and then **Santi Giovanni e Paolo** (▷ 53) and **Santa Maria dei Miracoli** (▷ 52). If you have time, walk to **Madonna dell'Orto** (▷ 48) and the **Ghetto** (▷ 56) in the city's quieter northern fringes.

Dinner Choose a restaurant in the San Polo or Dorsoduro districts, or in the streets around **Campo Santo Stefano**.

Evening Don't miss **Piazza San Marco** after dark, when Venice is even more magical than by day. After seeing the piazza, almost any walking itinerary will be rewarding. Or take the No. 1 or No. 82 *vaporetto* all the way down the **Grand Canal** just for the ride. If you don't have time for the boat ride today, be sure to leave time tomorrow.

ESSENTIAL VENICE TOP 25

▶ ▶ ▶

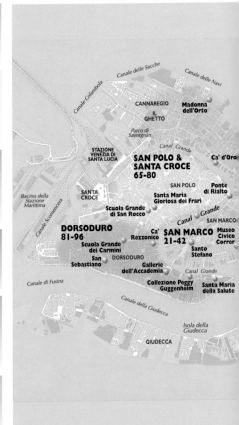

These pages are a quick guide to the Top 25, which are described in more detail later. Here they are listed alphabetically, and the tinted background shows which area they are in.

Ca' Rezzonico ▷ 84
Fine items from Venice's most hedonistic era are displayed in this museum.

Collezione Peggy Guggenheim ▷ 85
Modern art housed in an 18th-century *palazzo*.

Gallerie dell'Accademia ▷ 86–87 For the best in Venetian painting, be sure not to miss this gallery.

Madonna dell'Orto ▷ 48 Visit this unspoiled and tranquil Gothic church with its splendid art.

Murano ▷ 101 A miniature Venice and the home of Venetian glass production for over 800 years.

Museo Civico Correr ▷ 26–27 All about Venetian history and paintings.

Palazzo Ducale ▷ 28–29 One of the world's most beautiful buildings.

Piazza San Marco and Campanile ▷ 30–31 Stunning sights at every turn and great views from the Campanile.

San Giorgio Maggiore ▷ 102–103 Its campanile provides some of the best views of the city.

San Giovanni in Bragora ▷ 49 This small historic church has strong Vivaldi connections.

Santa Maria Gloriosa dei Frari ▷ 70–71
Venice's second largest church has great art.

Santa Maria Formosa ▷ 32 A Renaissance church set in a lovely *campo* in Castello.

Santi Giovanni e Paolo ▷ 53 The 'Pantheon of Venice' has some superb tombs and sculpture.

Shopping

Venice was one of the world's greatest trading hubs for 500 years before its decline in the 17th and 18th centuries. Sumptuous goods from all corners of the globe filled its markets, shops and warehouses. Today, its trade is less exotic but often still tempting.

Limited Choice
You will still find many designer names plus some great Italian fashion, accessories, shoes and other leatherware. But this is not a city to compare with other Italian hubs such as Rome, Milan or Florence. Space in the city is at a premium, so choice is relatively limited, and transport costs mean prices in shops are often higher than elsewhere.

Traditional Gifts
This said, Venice's extraordinary history has bequeathed the city several unique shopping possibilities. The artisan traditions of Murano and Burano, for example, make glass and lace from these two lagoon islands good buys—though you need to be on your guard against inferior, foreign-produced products. Glass trinkets can also provide some of Venice's most kitsch souvenirs.

Beautiful Masks
With the revival of the Venice carnival in 1979, the last few years has seen shops selling and producing the traditional masks (*maschere*) worn by celebrants proliferating. Some masks

---

BURANO LACE

Although lace was made by women of all classes during the Middle Ages, it was the development of an intricate stitch known as Burano point that made the eponymous island (▷ 106) famous for its lace. Mass production in the 19th century devastated the industry, and today only a handful of women make lace by hand. Much of what you see for sale in Burano and the rest of Venice is foreign- or machine-made. For the real thing you will have to search long and hard and be prepared to pay.

Venice has it all—market stalls, prints and books, Murano Glass, gleaming gold and magical masks

are mass-produced—but often still beautiful—while others are painstakingly created by hand in workshops, such as Tragicomica (▷ 77) around the city. Locally produced masks fetch high prices, but they do make the most wonderful souvenirs.

Stationery Delights

Marbled paper, another traditional Venetian craft, has also enjoyed a revival since the 1970s and shops across the city sell a range of paper products. The craft is almost 1,000 years old, and spread from Japan to Persia and the Arab world during the Middle Ages. It reached Europe in about the 15th century. Mass-produced papers are perfectly good, but the best buys are authentic, made using old hand- and woodblock-printing techniques.

Delicate Materials

Shops selling a host of fine silks, damasks and other fabrics (▷ panel, 38) reflect the city's trading days. And as you'd expect in a city with such an illustrious artistic past, there are many antiques shops filled with beautiful paintings, prints and objets d'art (▷ panel, 39).

And to Eat

Food souvenirs include pasta in every shape and form, rice and polenta, olive oil, dried *porcini* (mushrooms), vinegars, spices and traditional Burano biscuits.

MURANO GLASS

Glass-making began in Venice in Roman times, but took off in the 13th century, when foundries were moved to Murano (▷ 101) to lessen the risk of fire. Today, the island is a key production area; though shops sell Murano glass everywhere in Venice, the best choice, and keenest prices, are on the island. With its ornate forms and many tints, Murano glass is an acquired taste but the huge variety of styles includes both contemporary and traditional designs. At its best, glass is one of the city's most distinctive buys.

Shopping by Theme

Whether you're looking for a department store, a quirky boutique, or something in between, you'll find it all in Venice. On this page shops are listed by theme. For a more detailed write-up, see the individual listings in Venice by Area.

ART/ANTIQUES

Bac Art Studio (▷ 94)
Paolo Scarpa (▷ panel, 39)

BOOKS/STATIONERY

Ebrù (▷ 38)
Fantoni (▷ 38)
Filippi Editore Venezia
   (▷ 38)
Gianni Basso (▷ 59)
Goldoni (▷ 38)
Legatoria Piazzesi (▷ 39)
Legatoria Polliero (▷ 77)
Libreria Toletta e Toletta
   Studio (▷ 94)
Paolo Olbi (▷ 39)
Il Papiro (▷ 39)

FABRICS

Colorcasa (▷ 76)
Trois (▷ 39)

FASHION

Balocoloc (▷ 76)
Barbieri Arabesque (▷ 59)
Coin (▷ panel, 59)
Emporio Armani (▷ 38)
Fiorella (▷ 38)
Hibiscus (▷ 77)
Laura Biagiotti (▷ 39)
Missoni (▷ 39)
Mistero (▷ 60)
Mori & Bozzi (▷ 60)
Valentino (▷ 39)

FOOD/DRINK

Aliani Gastronomia (▷ 76)
Ballarin (▷ 59)
La Cantina (▷ 76)
Cantina ad Canton (▷ 59)
Casa del Parmigiano
   (▷ 76)
Co-op (▷ 59)
Drogheria Mascari (▷ 76)
Erberia (▷ 77)
Gobbetti (▷ 94)
Mercarto di Rialto (▷ 77)
La Nave d'Oro (▷ 60)
Panificio Volpe (▷ 60)
Pantagruelica (▷ 94)
Pescheria (▷ 77)
Rosa Salva (▷ 60)
Vino... e Vini (▷ 60)

GLASS

Berengo (▷ 38)
L'Isola (▷ 38)
Jesurum (▷ 59)
Pauly (▷ 60)
Susanna & Marina Sent
   (▷ 94)

JEWELLERY/BEADS

Antichità (▷ 94)
Anticlea Antiquariato
   (▷ 59)
Missiaglia (▷ 39)
Nardi (▷ 39)

SOUVENIRS

Emilio Ceccato (▷ 76)
Le Forcole di Saverio
   Pastor (▷ 94)
Galleria Livio de Marchi
   (▷ 38)
Gilberto Penzo (▷ 77)
Mondo Nova (▷ 94)
Tragicomica (▷ 77)

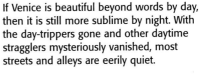

Venice by Night

If Venice is beautiful beyond words by day, then it is still more sublime by night. With the day-trippers gone and other daytime stragglers mysteriously vanished, most streets and alleys are eerily quiet.

Nighttime Enchantment

This is the time to stroll and take nightcaps in fusty, wooden-beamed bars. Wherever you walk you are rewarded by a fairy-tale world of medieval corners and views all the more magical for the cover of night. Much the same goes for Venice's watery domain, which is doubly enchanting on sultry summer evenings.

Quiet Entertainment

You need not fear for your personal security—Venice is very safe. You won't find clubs, pubs and thumping music: the city goes to bed remarkably early—one reason for the magical quiet of the streets. If you want some life, however, and the promise of an apéritif at the end of your stroll, you will find the odd late-night bar or evening recital, particularly around Campo Santa Margherita—and the city's opera and Casinò are both nighttime preferences—but such diversions are the exception rather than the rule. Venice by night is when the city is returned to itself, and when you can pretend, should you wish, that you are all but alone in the most beautiful place on earth. (See individual area chapters for further details of where to go for evening entertainment.)

After a view of Venice by night enjoy a cocktail at one of the city's sleek and atmospheric bars

DARK WATERS

Few things are more enchanting than a trip down the Grand Canal under a starlit sky. Indeed, it is almost worth organizing your arrival in the city for nightfall, so that you can approach your hotel by *vaporetto* or water taxi under the cover of darkness: it may be the most memorable part of your trip. And if you are going to lavish a small fortune on a gondola ride, make sure it is at night. Better still, take it in the silent, dark-dappled canals away from the main waterways.

Eating Out

Food in Venice is glorious, but it can also be dire, so if you want to eat well, steer away from places offering a *menù turistico* and be prepared to pay more than you might expect. Venetian cooking is based on fish, game and vegetables, with the accent on fish and seafood.

When to Eat
Breakfast is usually served between 8am and 10am. Locals often pop into a bar on their way to work for a cappuccino and a freshly baked *brioche* (sweet pastry). Both lunch and dinner operate in Venice on two different timescales—one for locals and one for visitors. Locals tend to eat earlier, which tends to prove cheaper, although there is no guarantee.

Where to Eat
Venice, like many Italian cities, has a confusing array of differently named eating places. A *ristorante* tends to be expensive, whereas the *trattoria* is less formal, less expensive, and often family-run. Such places may not have a printed menu, and the waiter will simply reel off a list of what's on offer; many speak enough English to help you choose. *Osterie* were originally pretty basic, and some still are, but the appellation has also been adopted by some very trendy establishments and can be synonymous with excellent food and rustic elegance. *Pizzerie* in Venice tend to open all day rather than just in the evenings but a Venetian pizza won't usually be as good as those served in Rome or Naples.

WHAT TO EAT

A full Venetian meal is gargantuan—antipasti, a *primo* (first course) of soup, rice or pasta, a *secondo* (main course) of fish with vegetable *contorni* (side dishes), then *formaggi* (cheese) and *dolce* (pudding). Do as the locals do and pick and mix. Few Venetians eat either cheese or pudding in restaurants, preferring to head for a *pasticceria* or choose a *gelato* (ice cream) if they want something sweet to round off a meal.

Surely one of the joys of Venice is a drink or a meal outside, either by a canal or in a picturesque square

Restaurants by Cuisine

There are restaurants to suit all tastes and budgets in Venice. On this page they are listed by cuisine. For a more detailed description of each restaurant, see Venice by Area.

CAFÉS/BARS

Boldrin (▷ 63)
Caffè Florian (▷ 41)
Caffé Lavena (▷ 40)
Causin (▷ 96)
Ciak (▷ 79)
Quadri (▷ 42)
Rosa Salva (▷ 42)

FINE DINING

Al Cova (▷ 63)
Al Mercanti (▷ 41)
Antica Montin (▷ 96)
Antico Martini (▷ 41)
La Caravella (▷ 41)
Da Fiore (▷ 79)
Do Forni (▷ 41)
Harry's Bar (▷ 42)
Harry's Dolci (▷ 96)
Post Vecie (▷ 80)
La Terrazza (▷ 64)

FISH/SEAFOOD

Al Conte Pescaor (▷ 41)
Al Mascaron (▷ 63)
Al Promessi Sposi (▷ 63)
Corte Sconta (▷ 63)
Da Ignazio (▷ 79)
Fiaschetteria Toscana (▷ 64)
Naranzaria (▷ 80)

ICE CREAM

Nico (▷ 96)
Paolin (▷ 42)

ITALIAN

Antica Birraria la Corte (▷ 79)
Rosticceria San Bartolomeo (▷ 42)

PIZZERIA

Alle Nono Risorte (▷ 79)
Alle Oche (▷ 79)
Il Refolo (▷ 80)

TRATTORIAS/OSTERIAS

Alla Rivetta (▷ 63)
Da Remigio (▷ 64)
Fiore (▷ 42)
Osteria al Bacareto (▷ 42)
Osteria alle Testiere (▷ 64)
Osteria la Zucca (▷ 80)
Osteria Oliva Nera (▷ 64)
Trattoria San Tomà (▷ 80)

VENETIAN

Ai Trei Spiedi (▷ 63)
Alla Madonna (▷ 79)
Le Bistrot de Venise (▷ 41)
La Bitta (▷ 96)
Dona Onesta (▷ 96)
Ribó (▷ 80)
Taverna San Trovaso (▷ 96)
Vini Da Gigio (▷ 64)
Vivaldi (▷ 80)

If You Like ...

However you'd like to spend your time in Venice, these top suggestions should help you tailor your ideal visit. Each sight or listing has a fuller write-up elsewhere in the book.

FABULOUS VIEWS

Take the elevator to the top of the Campanile (▷ 31) for views over the rooftops.
The bell-tower of San Giorgio Maggiore (▷ 102–103) offers sweeping vistas across the entire city.
Climb the tower of the cathedral on Torcello (▷ 104) for a panorama of the Venetian lagoon.

BURNING THE MIDNIGHT OIL

Have a drink in one of the cafés and bars on Campo Santa Margherita (▷ 91).
Find a fusty old *enoteca* (wine bar) such as Do Mori (▷ 78).
Venice has few late-opening nightspots—Vino Vino (▷ 40) and Paradiso Perduto (▷ 62) are two of the best.

Stunning views, sleek bars, historic tearooms and pleasant gardens—some of the joys of the city

THE LAP OF LUXURY

Splash out on a hotel on the Grand Canal (▷ 68–69); try the Gritti Palace (▷ 112).
Enjoy an expensive coffee or, better, an apéritif or late drink in Caffè Florian (▷ 41), a Venetian institution.
Go to a celebrity bar. It's crowded and a bit touristy, but Harry's Bar (▷ 42) still serves a fine cocktail.

A BREATH OF FRESH AIR

The tiny Giardini ex Reali (▷ 34) offers a little green space close to San Marco.
Visit Torcello (▷ 104) for some bracing sea air.
The cemetery island the Isola di San Michele (▷ 57) has plenty of room in which to stretch your legs.

Kids love dressing up for the annual Carnevale

KEEPING THE CHILDREN HAPPY

Take them on plenty of boat rides, especially down the Grand Canal (▷ 68–69).

Buy them a mask from Mondo Novo (▷ 94) or ice cream from Nico (▷ 96) or Causin (▷ 96).

Visit one of Murano's glass factories to see glassblowers in action (▷ 101).

SAVING FOR A RAINY DAY

Buy the Chorus Pass (€8) for reduced admission to some of Venice's finest churches (▷ panel, 4).

For the price of a boat ticket you can travel the length of the Grand Canal, surely the world's finest journey by public transport (▷ 118).

Just €0.60 on a *traghetto* (▷ 119) across the Grand Canal buys you a ride on a gondola.

Take to the water–the best way to see the sights of Venice

SPECIALTY SHOPPING

Many of Venice's high-fashion and other designer stores cluster in and around Calle Larga XXII Marzio. Check out Laura Biagiotti (▷ 39), one of the biggest and most popular names in Italian fashion.

For superb food shopping nothing beats the Rialto markets (▷ 74, 77) and the delicatessens in the surrounding streets such as Ruga Vecchia di San Giovanni.

Small, specialist stores line the Mercerie (▷ 34) and other streets between St. Mark's and the Rialto Bridge. Marbled paper, glass and local foods are popular choices.

Check out the amazing designs and brilliant tones of Venetian glass

ROMANTIC SUPPERS

Go on a boat trip to Isola di San Michele or take a swim at the Hotel Cipriani

Dine outdoors in summer—almost any restaurant or pizzeria will do. Try Da Ignazio (▷ 79).
Al Cova (▷ 63) may be expensive but the food is very good and the surroundings attractive.
Take a boat trip to Burano (▷ 106) and dine at one of the pretty little fish restaurants.

A MEMORABLE PLACE TO STAY

The Bauer (▷ 112) is one of Venice's most sumptuous and recently upgraded luxury hotels.
Little beats the old-world elegance of the Gritti Palace (▷ 112).
Amiable service and a peaceful position distinguish the Cipriani, one of Venice's luxury hotels of choice (▷ panel, 112).

AN EVENING ON THE TOWN

Take in an opera or concert at La Fenice (▷ 35, 40), Venice's opera house.
Contact the tourist office (▷ 119) to find a concert in one of Venice's churches or palaces.
Dress up for an evening's lighthearted gambling in Venice's casino (▷ 61).

A TASTE OF TRADITION

Take a gamble at the Grand Casino (above)

Antico Montin (▷ 96) has long been a pre-ferred haunt of artists and writers—it also has a delightful garden for summer dining.
The 18th-century dining rooms of Antico Martini (▷ 41) are the epitome of old-world Venetian elegance.
Bustling Alla Madonna (▷ 79) preserves the look and feel of an old-world Venetian *trattoria*.

The magical Rialto Bridge at night (right)

Venice by Area

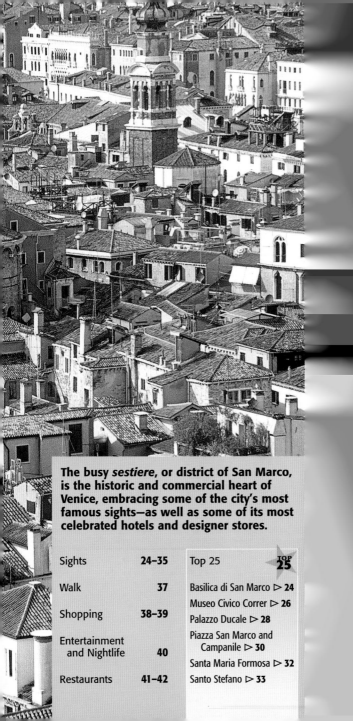

The busy *sestiere*, or district of San Marco, is the historic and commercial heart of Venice, embracing some of the city's most famous sights—as well as some of its most celebrated hotels and designer stores.

4

5

Rialto

Rialto

Palazzo
Dolfin-Mani

Palazzo
Dandolo

Canal
Grande

Palazzo
Bembo

Palazzo Corner
Martinengo

Palazzo
Farsetti

C te
Teatro

Teatro
Goldoni

Palazzo
Loredan

Palazzo
Grimani

Palazzo
Contarini
dei Cavalli

San
Benedetto

Mercerie

S Luca

Palazzo
Benzon

Campo
S Benedetto

Campo S Luca

Campo d Magaz

Sant Angelo

Palazzo
Curti
Palazzo
Corner-Spinelli

Teatro
Rossini

Campo
Manin

San Paterniar

S Ungheran

Ramo d Teatro

Museo
Fortuny

Campo
San Angelo

Oratio
dell'Annunziata

Palazzo
Contarini
del Boyolo

SAN
MARCO

Ateneo
Veneto

San Tomà

Palazzo
Contarini
delle Figure

Palazzo
Mocenigo

6

Palazzo
Da Lezze

Palazzo
Morolin

Palazzo
Grassi

San
Samuele

San
Samuele

Campo
S Samuele

Campiello
Novo

S Fantin

Campo
San Fantin

Teatro
La Fenice

Santo
Stefano

San
Maurizio

Puntolaguna

Palazzo
Malipiero

Ca' del
Duca

San Samuele

Campo Santo
Stefano

Campo
S Maurizio

Santa Maria
del Giglio

San Moisè

Campo
S Moisè

Larga XXII Marzo

Palazzo Falier

San Vidal

Palazzo
Giustinian
Lolin

Campo
Pisani

Palazzo
Bellavite

Campo
S Vidal

Palazzo
Franchetti

Palazzo
Pisani

Palazzo
Barbaro

Campo
S Maria
del Giglio

Palazzo Pisani
Gritti

Ponte
dell'Accademia

Palazzo
Barbaro

Palazzo Corner
(Ca' Grande)

S Maria
del Giglio

Palazzo
Flangini

Palazzo
Contarini
Fasan

Palazzo
Tiepolo

Palazzo
Treves
Bonfili

Palazzo
Zaguri

Santa Maria
del Giglio

Canal Grande

7

8

F

G

Ponte
di Rialto

Fondaco
dei Tedeschi

Palazzo
Bragadin
Carabba

Campo di
S Marina

Palazzo
Marcello

Palazzo
Donà

Palazzo
Priuli

San Lio

Santa Maria
della Fava

San
Salvador

Palazzo
Faccanon

Santa Maria
Formosa

Fondazione
Querini
Stampalia

Palazzo
Grimani

Campo
Santa Maria
Formosa

Palazzo
Tasca-Papafava

Palazzo
Soranzo

San
Zulian

S Giovanni
in Oleo

Palazzo
Trevisan

Campo
S S Filippo
e Giacomo

Torre dell'
Orologio

Procuratie
Vecchie

Palazzo
Patriarcale

Museo Diocesano
d'Arte Sacra

Piazza
San Marco

Basilica di
San Marco

P.tta del
Leoni

Caffè
Quadri

Campanile

Museo Civico
Correr

Caffè
Florian

Museo
Archeologico

Palazzo
Ducale

PONTE
DEI SOSPIRI

Palazzo
Dandolo

Palazzo
Prigioni

PONTE
DEL VIN

Procuratie
Nuove

Palazzo
Reale

Piazzetta
San Marco

Libreria
Sansoviniana

PONTE
DELLA
PAGLIA

Giardini
ex Reali

Zecca

S Teodoro

Leone di
San Marco

San Zaccaria
(Piazza San Marco)

Capitaneria
di Porto

Ridotto

San Marco

Palazzo
Giustinian

San Marco
(Vallaresso)

Canale di San Marco

*Isola di San
Giorgio Maggiore*

0   200 m

0   200 yds

H   J   K

Basilica di San Marco   TOP 25

HIGHLIGHTS

- Central door
- Façade mosaics
- Bronze horses
- Rood screen
- Mosaic pavement
- Pala d'Oro
- Interior mosaics

TIPS

- Dress code: no shorts; women must cover shoulders and upper arms.
- To avoid long lines go early or late afternoon.

Don't allow yourself to be discouraged by the teeming crowds that engulf the Basilica di San Marco, as ultimately no one can remain unimpressed by what is surely one of the world's greatest medieval buildings.

St. Mark's resting place The Basilica was begun in 832 to house the body of St. Mark, stolen from Alexandria by Venetian merchants four years earlier. For almost 1,000 years it served as the doge's private 'chapel' and the city's spiritual heart, accumulating the decorative fruits of a millennium to emerge as the most exotic hybrid of Western and Byzantine architecture in Europe. The original building (destroyed by rioting) was replaced in 978 and again in 1094, the church from the latter date making up most of the one you see today.

The superb mosaics decorating the upper walls and the cupola (far left); a mosaic depicting the church itself (top left); the beautiful exterior illuminated at night (top right); details of the domes on the exterior (below left); the Lion of St. Mark (below middle); the four bronze horses brought from Constantinople in 1204 (below right)

Time to explore Admiring the Basilica's treasures is exhausting, partly because there are so many, and partly because the almost constant crowds make exploring a dispiriting business. Still, the building remains overwhelmingly striking; spend a few minutes taking in some of the exterior details before plunging inside. These include the *Translation of the Body of St. Mark to the Basilica* (1260–70) above the leftmost door, the west façade's only original mosaic (the rest are later copies) and the superb Romanesque carvings (1240–65) above the central door. Inside, see the famous bronze horses (probably 3rd century AD) in the upper gallery, the view from the Loggia dei Cavalli, the treasury (full of antique silverware), and the magnificent Pala d'Oro, an altar screen encrusted with over 2,600 pearls, rubies, emeralds and other precious stones.

THE BASICS

✚ J6
✉ Piazza San Marco 1, San Marco 30124
☎ 041 522 5205 or 041 522 5697
⏰ Apr–end Oct Mon–Sat 9.45–5.30, Sun 2–4; Nov–end Mar Mon–Sat 9.45–4.30, Sun 2–4
🍴 Piazza San Marco
🚏 All services to San Marco or San Zaccaria
♿ Some steps; uneven floors
💶 Basilica free. Treasury and Pala d'Oro expensive

Museo Civico Correr

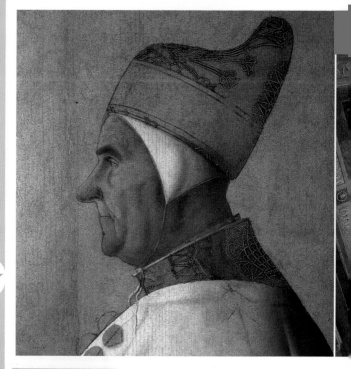

HIGHLIGHTS

- Aerial view of Venice (1500), Jacopo de' Barbari
- *Daedalus and Icarus*, Canova
- *Two Women*, Carpaccio
- *The Man in the Red Hat*, Lorenzo Lotto (attributed)
- *Pietà*, Antonello da Messina
- *Madonna and Child*, Giovanni Bellini

Probably only a fraction of the visitors thronging Piazza San Marco venture into the Museo Civico Correr. Those who do not are missing Venice's finest museum and picture gallery collections.

Fascinating overview Much of the Correr's collection was accumulated by Abbot Teodoro Correr, a Venetian worthy, and bequeathed to the city in 1830. Today, it spreads over three floors, devoted respectively to historical displays, an art gallery and the small Museo del Risorgimento (this details the 19th-century unification of Italy). The key rooms have lovely old prints and paintings of the city, followed by salons devoted to different episodes of Venetian history. Particularly outstanding are the rooms of costumes and hats, standards, armour, globes, old weapons and ships' instruments.

A portrait of Giovanni Mocenigo (1478–85), the Doge of Venice in 1467 painted by Gentile Bellini and on display on the upper floor of the Museo Civico Correr (left); the beautiful ceiling of the entrance hall to the museum has striking art and superbly executed stucco work (right)

Perhaps the most memorable section, however, is the footwear display showing the famous 'platform' shoes once worn by Venetian ladies of rank.

More art One of the main sections of the museum consists of a large hall devoted to several fine sculptures by Antonio Canova. Look out, in particular, for the touching study of Daedalus fixing a pair of flimsy wings to Icarus's arms. Occupying the top floor is the city's second-finest art gallery after the Accademia. Its most popular picture is Carpaccio's *Two Women* (1507), a masterful study of ennui once known as *The Courtesans* for the plunging necklines. Other well-known paintings include *The Man in the Red Hat* (by either Carpaccio or Lorenzo Lotto) and a *Pietà* by Antonello da Messina, and works by Cosmè Tura, Alvise Vivarini, and Jacopo, Giovanni and Gentile Bellini.

THE BASICS

www.museicivicivenezia ni.it
H6
Procuratie Nuove, Ala Napoleonica, Piazza San Marco 52, San Marco 30124
041 240 5211
Apr–end Oct daily 9–7; Nov–end Mar 9–5 (last ticket sold 1 hour earlier)
Piazza San Marco
Vallaresso N, 1, 2
Poor
Expensive (joint Piazza San Marco ticket)

Palazzo Ducale

HIGHLIGHTS

- Bridge of Sighs
- Tetrarchs
- Porta della Carta
- Scala dei Giganti
- Arco Foscari
- Sala dell'Anticollegio
- Sala del Collegio
- Sala del Maggior Consiglio
- Armoury and prisons

TIP

- Winter visitors should dress warmly as there is no heating and it can be very cold.

Italy has a host of beautiful Gothic buildings, but the Palazzo Ducale is by far the most captivating: the seat of the doge and home to Venice's various offices of state for almost a thousand years.

Evolution The first ducal palace, completed in 814, was a severe fortress built on one of the few clay redoubts in the lagoon. This burned down in 976, as did its successor in 1106. By 1419 the palace was in its third—and final—incarnation. Three years later, the great hall, or Sala del Maggior Consiglio, was completed—one of many additions made to the interior. By 1550 most work had been completed, only to be undone by fires in 1574 and 1577, conflagrations that not only destroyed masterpieces by some of Venice's greatest painters, but also threatened the entire

The Scala del'Oro, the gold staircase, inside the Palazzo Ducale (far left); statue of Atlas (top left); the striking façade of the palace, home to the doges of Venice (top right); the main entrance to the palace (below right); two of the mysterious Tetrarch sculptures (below middle); the fabulous Sala del Maggior Consiglio (below right)

building with collapse. Restoration work continued on and off until the 1880s.

Details Outside, note the famous Ponte dei Sospiri (Bridge of Sighs), tucked down a canal at the palace's eastern end, and the fine sculptures on each of the building's three corners. Also take in the excellent carving of the pillars and capitals, and the palace's superb main doorway, the Porta della Carta (1438–43), together with the famous little group of red porphyry knights, or tetrarchs, to its left. An ornate staircase leads up several flights to the beginning of the palace's set itinerary, a marked route leading from one lavishly designed room to the next. Look for works by Tintoretto, Veronese and other Venetian masters. Tintoretto's gargantuan *Paradiso* (1588–92), the world's largest oil painting is in the Sala del Maggior Consiglio.

THE BASICS

www.museicivicineveneziani.it

➕ J6

✉ Piazzetta San Marco, San Marco 30124

☎ Palace and booking for guided tours 041 271 5911 or 041 520 9070

🕐 Palace Apr–end Oct daily 9–7 (last ticket sold 6); Nov–end Mar daily 9–5

🍴 Palace café

🚃 All services to San Zaccaria or San Marco

♿ Poor: steps to upstairs

💰 Expensive (joint Piazza San Marco ticket)

Piazza San Marco and Campanile

DID YOU KNOW?

● Number of Venetian towers in 1650: 200
● Number today: 170
● Number that have collapsed: 30
● Number of Campanile bells: 5
● The Maleficio bell tolled during executions
● The Nona bell tolled at noon
● The Marangona bell tolled at the start and end of the working day
● All bells tolled at the election of a pope or doge
● Prisoners were hung in cages from the Campanile
● Elevator added in 1962

HIGHLIGHTS

Piazza
● Basilica di San Marco (▷ 24–25)
● Palazzo Ducale (▷ 28–29)
● Museo Civico Correr (▷ 26–27)
● Procuratie
● Libreria Sansoviniana
● Torre dell'Orologio (▷ 35)
● Zecca
● Caffè Florian (▷ 41)

Avoid visiting Piazza San Marco on your first morning as the crowds might turn you against Venice. When you do visit, arrive early to beat the crowds to see the Basilica, Palazzo Ducale and Campanile.

Hordes Europe's 'drawing room' was how Napoleon described Venice's main square, though glancing at today's crowds he would probably be less complimentary. Arrive early or in the evening, however—or off-season—and the piazza can still work its considerable charms. Over and above the obvious sights and (expensive) cafés, make a point of taking in the Zecca (mint), the Procuratie (administrative offices), the underrated Museo Civico Correr, and the Libreria Sansoviniana, considered one of the greatest buildings of its day. Also see the Torre dell'Orologio (▷ 35) and

Feeding the pigeons in Piazza San Marco (far left); St. Theodore atop his pillar in the square (top left); view from the top of the Campanile down to Quadri café (top middle); the five striking domes of the Basilica (below left); the soaring Campanile (below middle); looking down to the canal beyond Piazza San Marco (right)

notice the two granite columns on the waterfront besides the Palazzo Ducale.

Campanile You'll almost certainly need to wait in line for the tiny elevator to the top, but it's worth it for the views from this detached belltower of the Basilica di San Marco. On a clear day they stretch as far as the Alps. Venice's tallest building (98.5m/323ft) was reputedly begun in 912 on 25 April, the feast day of St. Mark. Over the years, however, erosion and shallow foundations (just 20m/66ft deep) proved the tower's undoing, and it collapsed on 14 July 1902, though with no casualties. It was rebuilt, as the Venetians insisted, *dov'era e com'era* —'where it was and how it was'—and inaugurated on 25 April 1912, exactly 1,000 years after its predecessor. This time, though, it was 650 tons lighter and was supported by an extra 1,000 foundation piles.

THE BASICS

www.museicivicivenezian.it
🔲 H6–J6
☎ Museo Archeologico
041 522 5978
🕐 Museo Archeologico
Apr–end Oct daily 9–7;
Nov–end Mar daily 9–5
🍴 Caffè Florian (▷ 41)
and Quadri (▷ 42)
🚤 Vallaresso N, 1, 2, 4, or
all services to San Zaccaria
🚹 Good
🏛 Museo Archeologico
moderate
Campanile
☎ 0141 522 4064
🕐 Jul–end Aug daily 9–9;
Apr–end Jun, Sep–end
Oct; Nov–end Mar daily
9.30–4.15
🚹 Poor: narrow access to
elevator
🏛 Expensive

Santa Maria Formosa

Sublime art (left); exterior grotesque (middle); Campo Santa Maria Formosa (right)

THE BASICS

➕ J5

✉ Campo Santa Maria Formosa, Castello 5263

☎ 041 275 0462

🕐 Mon–Sat 10–5, Sun 1–5

🚏 Campo Santa Maria Formosa

🚤 Rialto or Fondamente Nuove N, 1, 2, 4, 41, 42, 51, 52

♿ Good

💵 Inexpensive

❓ Chorus Pass (▷ 4)

HIGHLIGHTS

● Façades
● Martial bas-reliefs
● Plaque recording 1916 incendiary bomb
● Campanile's stone mask
● Interior
● *Madonna della Misericordia*, Bartolomeo Vivarini
● *Santa Barbara*, Palma il Vecchio

Santa Maria Formosa's appeal rests partly on its surrounding square. An archetypal Venetian *campo*, it is a pleasantly rambling affair, full of local vibrancy and lined with attractive cafés and palaces.

The structure This church takes its name from una *Madonna formosa*, a 'buxom Madonna', which appeared to St. Magnus in the 7th century, instructing him to follow a small white cloud and build a church wherever it settled. The present building, completed in 1492, was grafted onto an 11th-century Byzantine church, from which it borrowed its Greek-Cross plan, a common feature of Byzantine (and later) churches dedicated to the Virgin. The façade (1542) was paid for by the Cappello family, hence its statue of Vincenzo Cappello, a Venetian admiral. Note the carved face on the bell tower to the left, one of Venice's most famous grotesques.

Interior The church's interior is a unique blend of Renaissance decoration and ersatz Byzantine cupolas, barrel vaults and narrow-columned screens. Of particular interest are two paintings, the first being Bartolomeo Vivarini's *Madonna della Misericordia* (1473), a triptych in the first chapel on the right (south) side. It was financed by the church's congregation, depicted in the picture sheltering beneath the Virgin's protective cloak. The second, and more famous picture, Palma il Vecchio's *Santa Barbara* (1522–24), depicts the patron saint of artillerymen, and portrays the artist's daughter as its model.

Tomb of Doge Francisco Morosini (left); interior detail of Santo Stefano (right)

Santo Stefano

Delight in the sensation of walking from the heat and bustle of a city into a building that induces immediate calm, an effect gained by the soothing Gothic interior of this, one of Venice's loveliest churches.

Ideally placed Santo Stefano sits on the edge of Campo Santo Stefano (also known as Campo Francesco Morosini), one of Venice's most charming squares; the nearby Paolin (▷ 42) is an ideal place to sit with a drink or ice cream. The church has not always been so peaceful, having been re-consecrated six times to wash away the stain of blood spilled by murders within its walls. Today, its interior is overarched by an exquisite 'ship's keel' ceiling and framed by tie beams and pillars of Greek and red Veronese marble.

Final resting place At the middle of the nave lies Doge Francesco Morosini (d1612, and buried under Venice's largest tomb slab), famous for recapturing the Peloponnese and blowing up the Parthenon with a single shot. Other tombs command attention, notably Pietro Lombardo's *Monument to Giacomo Surian* (d1493) on the wall to the right of the main door, but the church's chief artistic interest lies in the gloomy sacristy at the end of the right nave. The altar wall displays two narrow-framed Saints by Bartolomeo Vivarini, as well as a recessed 13th-century Byzantine icon. On the walls to either side are four paintings by Tintoretto and four portraits of Augustinian cardinals, displayed here as Santo Stefano is an Augustinian church.

THE BASICS

🔲 G6
✉ Campo Santo Stefano (Campo Francesco Morosini) Castello 2774
☎ 041 275 0462 or 041 275 0494
🕐 Mon–Sat 10–5, Sun 1–5
🍴 Campo Santo Stefano
🚤 San Samuele or Sant' Angelo N, 1, 2, 4
♿ Very good
💷 Inexpensive
❓ Chorus Pass (▷ 4)

HIGHLIGHTS

● Portal statues, Bartolomeo Bon
● Ceiling
● Tomb of Doge Morosini
● Tomb of Giovanni Gabriele, first altar on left
● *Monument to Giacomo Surian*, Pietro Lombardo
● *Madonna and Child with Saints*, Bonifaccio
● *Saints*, Bartolomeo Vivarini
● Tintoretto paintings
● *Monument to Giovanni Falier*, Antonio Canova

More to See

GIARDINI EX REALI

About the only patch of green in the vicinity of Piazza San Marco is the Giardini ex Reali, a waterfront oasis of trees behind the Procuratie Nuove. Benches are shaded by trees and the view over the Bacino di San Marco is superb but the downsides are the constant crowds and the tightly packed rows of souvenir stalls.

✚ H6–J6 ✉ San Marco ⛴ San Marco N, 1, 2 or Vallaresso ✋ Free

THE MERCERIE

The *calli* known as the Mercerie are Venice's busiest shopping streets, where you'll find everything from fashion to shops specializing in just one particular item such as hats.

✚ H5 ⛴ Rialto N, 1, 2, 4

MUSEO DIOCESANO D'ARTE SACRA

This museum exhibits works of art removed from Venice's deconsecrated churches. Its chief treasure, however, is the 12th-century exquisite cloister of Sant'Apollonia in whose buildings it's housed. Venice's only example of Romanesque architecture.

✚ J6 ✉ Chiostro di Sant'Apollonia, Sant' Apollonia, Castello 4312 ☎ 041 277 0561 or 041 522 9166 🕐 Daily 10.30–12.30 ✋ By donation ⛴ All services to San Zaccaria

PALAZZO CONTARINI DE BOVOLO

www.scalabovolo.org

The Gothic Palazzo Contarini del Bovolo is best known for its sinuous exterior staircase. Such staircases are called *scale a chiocciola* (snail stairs) in Italian—the Venetian dialect for snail is *bovolo*. The beautiful redbrick and Istrian stone stair gives access on five different levels to graceful loggias curving around inside a tower.

✚ G6 ✉ Calle dei Risi, San Marco ☎ 041 270 2464 🕐 Apr–end Oct daily 10–6; Nov–end Mar Sat–Sun 10–4 ✋ Inexpensive ⛴ Rialto N, 1, 2

PALAZZO GRASSI

www.palazzograssi.it

Outside, nothing could be more traditionally 18th-century classical than this

Palazzo Contarini del Bolovo

Relaxing in the Giardini ex Reali

palace. Inside, it's another story; the interior was converted in the 1980s by Gianni Agnelli of Fiat to become Venice's most high-profile exhibition venue. In 2004, following the death of Agnelli, it was bought by François Pinault, the French millionaire collector and owner of a business empire that includes Gucci, Yves Saint Laurent and Christie's, who is slowly moving his collection of 20th-century art to Venice.

➕ F6 ✉ Campo San Samuele, San Marco 3231 ☎ 041 523 1680 🚤 San Samuele N, 2

SAN MAURIZIO

Rebuilt in the early 19th century and hardly used in the 20th, San Maurizio found a new role in 2004 when it opened as a Vivaldi exhibition area. The chief draw is the fine collection of old musical instruments, whose sound provides the music that's a constant backdrop to your visit. You can buy CDs, tapes and DVDs relating to the composer.

➕ G6 ✉ Campo San Maurizio, San Marco ☎ 041 241 1840 ⏰ Varies with exhibition ✋ Free 🚤 Giglio 1

TEATRO LA FENICE

www.teatrolafenice.it

Fenice is the Italian word for phoenix, and Venice's opera house, designed by Giannantonio Selva in 1792, rose from the ashes of the disastrous fire of 1996 to reopen for the 2004–5 season. The new hall is a delight. Book well in advance for performances or join one of the regular tours.

➕ G6 ✉ Campo San Fantin, San Marco 1965 ☎ 041 786 611 ⏰ Guided visits only, bookable in advance in person or by tel, fax or internet 🚤 Giglio 1

TORRE DELL'OROLOGIO

San Marco's clock tower was built between 1496 and 1506. The exterior stone dial shows the 24 hours in Roman numerals, with the interior face showing the signs of the zodiac and phases of the moon.

➕ J6 ✉ Piazza San Marco, San Marco 30124 ☎ 041 520 9070 (reservations compulsory) ⏰ Guided visits in English Mon–Wed 10, 11, 1, Thu–Sun 2, 3, 5 ✋ Expensive (with Piazza San Marco joint ticket) 🚤 Vallaresso N, 1, 2 and all services to San Zaccaria

The striking Palazzo Grassi

Sublime art in San Maurizio

Around San Marco

San Marco is the heart of Venice, packed with narrow alleys, light-filled squares and fine *palazzi*, churches, workshops and stores.

DISTANCE: 2.5km (1.5 miles) **ALLOW:** 1.5–2 hours

START

PONTE DI RIALTO
✛ H5 🚏 Rialto N, 1, 2

END

PONTE DI RIALTO
✛ H5 🚏 Rialto N, 1, 2

① From the Rialto Bridge walk to Campo San Bartolomeo. Turn right on Via II Aprile. Pass San Salvador and continue on Calle dell'Ovo and Calle Teatro Goldoni.

⑧ Follow Mercería San Zulian and Mercería San Salvatore back to Via II Aprile, which brings you back to the Rialto Bridge.

② Turn right into Campo San Luca and on into Campo Manin. Take the alley off the *campo* south to see the Palazzo Contarini del Bovolo (▷ 34). Return to the *campo*.

⑦ Bear left past San Moisè and turn left up Calle Frezzeria. Take the second right (Calle Salvadego) and walk into Piazza San Marco (▷ 30–31) with all its famous sights. Take Mercería dell'Orologio out of the square and the third right to San Zulian.

③ Bear left (west) along Calle Cortesia. Turn left on Calle dei Assassini-Calle Verona to Campo San Fantin. Follow Calle Fenice.

⑥ Return to the *campo* and take Calle Spezier right (east) out of the square. Walk through Campo San Maurizio and past the church of Santa Maria del Giglio into Calle Larga XXII Marzo.

④ View the Fenice opera house (▷ 35) alongside. Take the first right through Campiello Fenice and on into Campo Sant'Angelo. Visit Santo Stefano (▷ 33).

⑤ Go down Campo Stefano to Ponte dell'Accaccdemia (▷ 92) for the view.

Shopping

BERENGO
www.berengo.com
This smart gallery presents glass as sculptural fine art, including some strange and striking pieces that may not be for all tastes. There is the chance to visit another showroom on Murano (▷ 101) at Fondamenta dei Vetrai.
🞣 J6 ✉ Calle Larga San Marco, San Marco 412–413 ☎ 041 241 0763 🚏 All services to San Marco or San Zaccaria

EBRÛ
The owner of this shop, Alberto Valese, was at the cutting edge of the 1970s revival in Venetian marbled paper. His shop takes its name from the traditional Turkish marbling technique used to create many of his products. Some of the smaller items make ideal gifts or souvenirs.
🞣 F6 ✉ Campo Santo Stefano, San Marco 3471 ☎ 041 523 8830 🚏 Giglio 1

EMPORIO ARMANI
No leading Italian city would be complete without a flagship store dedicated to one of the most famous names in Italian fashion. In Venice Armani is on one of the city's main shopping streets. The clothes are peerless, classic and exquisitely cut. Always worth a look around.
🞣 H6 ✉ Calle dei Fabbri, San Marco 989 ☎ 041 523 7808 🚏 Rialto N, 1, 2

FANTONI
This well-known shop contains the city's largest selection of big, glossy art books.
🞣 H5 ✉ Salizzada San Luca, San Marco 4119 ☎ 041 522 0700 🚏 Rialto N, 1, 2

FILIPPI EDITORE VENEZIA
This specialist shop is renowned for its large collection of books on all aspects of Venice (mostly in Italian) and its many facsimile editions of old books.
🞣 J5 ✉ Calle della Casselleria, San Marco 5284 ☎ 041 523 6916 🚏 Rialto N, 1, 2, 4

FIORELLA
www.fiorellagallery.com
Hilarious and wonderfully original, Fiorella has Venice's best-dressed window: the shop dummies, crafted in wood, represent

MARIANO FORTUNY
Fortuny was born in Catalonia, Spain in 1871, the son of a painter and fabric collector. He moved to Venice when he was 18, soon gaining renown in fields ranging from physics and chemistry to architecture and theatre design. Today, he is best remembered for his fabrics, and in particular for the pleated dresses he created that were so fine they could be rolled up and threaded through a wedding ring.

life-size models of former doges, each decked out in high heels and other slightly offbeat high fashion items.
🞣 F6 ✉ Campo Santo Stefano (Campo Francesco Morosini), San Marco 2806 ☎ 041 520 9228 🚏 Accademia N, 1, 2

GALLERIA LIVIO DE MARCHI
www.liviodemarchi.com
You will probably see examples of Livio de Marchi's work as you walk around Venice: everyday objects such as socks, umbrellas or hanging shirts lovingly and precisely carved of wood. You may not want to buy the items, but the works are unique—and great fun.
🞣 F6 ✉ Salizzada San Samuele, San Marco 3157/a ☎ 041 528 5694 🚏 Sant'Angelo or San Samuele N, 1, 2, 4

GOLDONI
Well stocked and by common consent the best general bookshops in the city, Goldini has a wide range of literature on the city, along with a limited selection of English and other foreign-language titles.
🞣 H5 ✉ Calle dei Fabbri, San Marco 4742 ☎ 041 522 2384 🚏 Vallaresso N, 1, 2

L'ISOLA
Grotesque modern glass litters countless Venetian shops and souvenir stands. This shop has

SHOPPING

⊞

SAN MARCO

some of the city's better contemporary designs, although you may still find some of them too far-fetched. As with much Venetian glass, prices can be surprisingly high.
➕ H6 ✉ Salizzada San Moisè, San Marco 1468
☎ 041 523 1973
🚤 Vallaresso N, 1, 2

LAURA BIAGIOTTI
One of the big names in Italian fashion, in the heart of one of the city's most exclusive shopping streets, which runs west from Piazza San Marco.
➕ H6–G6 ✉ Calle Larga (Viale) XXII Marzo, San Marco 2400/a ☎ 041 520 3401
🚤 Vallaresso N, 1, 2

LEGATORIA PIAZZESI
Established in 1900, this is one of the last workshops in the city to use traditional wood-block methods to hand-print its exceptionally fine papers, books and stationery. Expensive.
➕ G6 ✉ Campiello della Feltrina, San Marco 2511
☎ 041 522 1202 🚤 Giglio 1

MISSIAGLIA
Missiaglia is considered the city's finest jeweller. White-and-yellow gold settings with tinted stones are the main specialty: Styles are mostly classic, but with occasional more contemporary pieces. With a Piazza San Marco setting, bargains are limited.
➕ H6 ✉ Procuratie Vecchie, Piazza San Marco 125

☎ 041 522 4464
🚤 Vallaresso N, 1, 2

MISSONI
www.missoni.com
Another big Italian fashion name, best known for brightly hued knitwear and similarly innovative linens and casualwear.
➕ H6–H7 ✉ Calle Vallaresso, San Marco 1312
☎ 041 520 5733
🚤 Vallaresso N, 1, 2

NARDI
www.nardijewellery.com
Rivals Missiaglia for the title of Venice's smartest jeweller. High prices.
➕ H6 ✉ Procuratie Nuove, Piazza San Marco 69, San Marco 30124 ☎ 041 522 5733 🚤 Vallaresso N, 1, 2

PAOLO OLBI
Another artisan at the forefront of the revival of marbled paper. Olbi's appealing shop sells an endless range of marbled stationery and ornaments

ANTIQUES
Bric-à-brac and antique bargains are rare in a city that is acutely aware of its past and the value of its *objets d'art*. Still, Venice provides an almost unlimited choice of beautiful things to buy. The most famous shops in San Marco are Paolo Scarpa's two outlets at Campo San Moisè, San Marco 1464 (➕ H6) and Calle Larga (Viale) XXII Marzo, San Marco 2089 (➕ H6).

that make the perfect gift.
➕ G6 ✉ Calle della Mandola, San Marco 3653
☎ 041 528 5025
🚤 Sant'Angelo 1, 2

IL PAPIRO
A fine little shop, with branches around the world, selling marbled paper as well as some handsome desk objects, cards, notebooks, diaries and other pretty stationery. There are two other outlets in the city.
➕ G6 ✉ Calle del Piovan, San Marco 2764 ☎ 041 522 3055 (all shops) 🚤 Giglio 1

TROIS
This beautiful old shop is the only place in Venice where you can still buy original Fortuny fabrics. Choose from stunning lengths down to cushion covers and browse among the beadwork, though elegance comes at a price.
➕ G6–G7 ✉ Campo San Maurizio, San Marco 2666
☎ 041 522 2905
🚤 Vallaresso N, 1, 2

VALENTINO
www.valentino.com
The doyen of Rome *alta moda* and stylish ready-to-wear clothes has a shop just west of Piazza San Marco, close to the stores of other leading names in the world of fashion.
➕ H6 ✉ Salizzada San Moisè, San Marco 1473
☎ 041 520 5733
🚤 Vallaresso N, 1, 2

Entertainment and Nightlife

AL VOLTO
Wood-beamed *enoteca* north of Campo Manin. Snacks and a staggering 1,300 different wines.
➕ G5 ✉ Calle Cavalli, San Marco 4081 ⏰ Mon–Sat 10–2.30, 5–10 🚤 Rialto N, 1, 2, 4

BACARO JAZZ
The fabulous Cuban *barista* (barman) here does his utmost to make you feel welcome, and more importantly mixes a mean *mojito*. Expect plenty of jazz and *gondolieri* enjoying themselves. There is good food, too.
➕ H5 ✉ Salizzada del Fontego dei Tedeschi, San Marco 5546 ☎ 041 528 5249 ⏰ Thu–Tue 4pm–3am
🚤 Rialto N, 1, 2

CAFFÉ LAVENA
www.lavena.it
This San Marco café is in the grand style like the Florian and the Quadri, but has never quite acquired their cult status. It offers just as good a place to hang out late at night. Dating back to 1750, it has long been a particular preference of gondoliers.
➕ H6 ✉ Piazza San Marco, San Marco 133 ☎ 041 522 4070 ⏰ Apr–end Nov daily 9.30am–12.30am; Dec–end Mar Wed–Mon 9.30am–10.30pm
🚤 Vallaresso N, 1, 2

HAIG'S BAR
Haig's is an American-style piano bar and part of the Giglio restaurant, popular with visiting Americans and young locals—and

those locals who wish they were younger! Very good, but slightly pricey, Venetian fare.
➕ G7 ✉ Campo Santa Maria del Giglio, San Marco 5277 ☎ 041 528 9456 ⏰ Daily 11.30–3, 7–2
🚤 Giglio 1

OSTERIA AGLI ASSASSINI
This wine bar is off the beaten track between Campo Manin and Campo Sant'Angelo, and has a good selection of wines, light snacks and basic meals.
➕ G6 ✉ Rio Terrà degli Assassini, San Marco 3695 ⏰ Closed Sat lunch and Sun
🚤 Sant'Angelo 1, 2

OSTERIA ALLE BOTTEGHE
Lively and very busy wine bar, just north of

WINE BARS
Old-fashioned wine bars, or *bacari*, are a Venetian way of life. One of the city's more civilized habits is the custom of breaking up the day with an *ombra* ('shadow'), a small glass of wine that takes its name from the idea of escaping the heat of the sun for a restorative tipple. A small snack, or *cichetto*, usually accompanies the drink. An *enoteca* is a more refined bar, with a greater choice of wines and a range of reasonably priced snacks and hot meals.

Campo Santo Stefano (Campo Francesco Morosini) offering plenty of wines and a small selection of snacks.
➕ F6 ✉ Calle delle Botteghe, San Marco 3454 ☎ 041 522 8181 ⏰ Mon–Sat 11–4, 7–10 🚤 Sant'Angelo or San Samuele 1, 2

TEATRO LA FENICE
www.teatrolafenice.it
This famous opera house (▷ 35) hosts a full schedule of operas and other concerts.
➕ G6 ✉ Campo San Fantin, San Marco 1965 ☎ 041 786 500; information 041 2424 or 041 786 511; for tickets www.hellovenezia.it or by fax 041 241 8028 🚤 Giglio 1

TORINO@NOTTE
Live jazz, beer, spritz and toasted sandwiches make up the staple diet of the fun-loving crowd here. The action spills out onto the *campo* during the summer and during carnival.
➕ H5 ✉ Campo San Luca, San Marco 459 ☎ 041 522 3914 ⏰ Tue–Sat 7.30pm–1am
🚤 Rialto N, 1, 2

VINO VINO
Rather more showy and smarter than some of Venice's humbler bars, this two-roomed spot close to the opera house has more than 100 different wines to accompany its snacks and meals.
➕ G6 ✉ Ponte delle Veste, Calle delle Veste, San Marco 2007a ☎ 041 241 7688 ⏰ Wed–Mon 10.30am–midnight 🚤 Giglio 1

Restaurants

PRICES

Prices are approximate, based on a 3-course meal for one person.
€€€   over €55
€€   €35–€55
€   under €35

AI MERCANTI (€€)

www.aimercanti.com
Ai Mercanti is not far from San Marco and the beautifully restored La Fenice hall. With tasteful dishes and elegant surroundings, it makes a perfect place to go after a night at a show. Dishes include *risotto alle vongole* and *spaghetti con melanzane e calamaretti*. Delightful terrace for summer dining.
⊞ H6 ⊠ Calle dei Fuseri, San Marco 4346/a ☎ 041 523 8269 ⊙ Closed Sun, Mon lunch ⊑ Rialto N, 1, 2, 4

AL CONTE PESCAOR (€€)

A wonderful tiny fish restaurant that caters to Venetians, despite its proximity to Piazza San Marco.
⊞ J6–H6 ⊠ Piscina San Zulian, San Marco 544 ☎ 041 522 1483 ⊙ Closed Sun and Jan in winter ⊑ Vallaresso N, 1, 2

ANTICO MARTINI (€€€)

www.anticomartini.com
Established in the 18th century, the Martini has long been one of the city's most stylish restaurants. Classic Venetian cuisine with seafood playing a key role. The terrace overlooks La Fenice (▷ 35), and the wine list numbers 300 labels. Meals are served until 1am, unusually late in Venice.
⊞ G6 ⊠ Campo San Fantin, San Marco 2007 ☎ 041 522 4121 ⊑ Giglio 1

LE BISTROT DE VENISE (€€)

www.bistrotdevenise.com
A wonderful place to know about if you want a late meal, in an artsy atmosphere, in a city where many restaurants close surprisingly early. Despite the name and the French look of the place, the menu is traditionally Venetian with dishes like

WINES

Most of Venice's wine comes from the Veneto region on the mainland. Its best-known wines are the usually unexceptional Soave (white), and Valpolicella and Bardolino (reds). More interesting whites include Soave Classico, Bianco di Custoza, Tocai, Pinot Grigio and the wines of the Breganze region. The best white of all is Prosecco, a delicious dry sparkling wine often drunk as an apéritif. Interesting reds include Raboso, the wines of the Colle Berici and Lison-Pramaggiore regions, and two excellent dessert wines: Amarone and Recioto della Valpolicella.

homemade tagliatelle with lagoon eel.
⊞ H5 ⊠ Callei dei Fabbri, San Marco 4685 ☎ 041 523 6651 ⊙ Daily noon–1am ⊑ Rialto N, 1, 2

CAFFÈ FLORIAN (€–€€€)

The oldest, prettiest and most expensive of Venice's famous cafés has been serving customers since 1720. Prices are high, but treat yourself at least once for the experience and the chance to admire the lovely frescoed and mirrored interior.
⊞ H6 ⊠ Piazza San Marco, San Marco 56–59 ⊙ Closed Wed ⊑ Vallaresso N, 1, 2

LA CARAVELLA (€€€)

The interior of this restaurant, one of two in the Saturnia hotel, is decked out in the manner of a Venetian galley. The over-the-top decor fails to detract from the normally outstanding food, but it can be prone to lapses. The cooking has international as well as Venetian touches.
⊞ G6–H6 ⊠ Calle Larga (Viale) XXII Marzo, San Marco 2398 ☎ 041 520 8901 ⊑ Giglio 1

DO FORNI (€€€)

A slightly self-conscious restaurant known as one of the places to eat among locals and visitors alike. One dining room is furnished rustically and the other fashioned like

an opulent Orient Express cabin. The number of tables and the menu have grown with the restaurant's success, but despite the chaos the food remains good—although at inflated prices.

J6 Calle dei Specchieri, San Marco 468 041 523 2148 Vallaresso N, 1, 2

FIORE (€€)

This thoroughly local *trattoria* is full of life, with a popular bar serving snacks as well as an intimate restaurant. Be careful not to confuse it with Da Fiore in San Polo (▷ 79). It is just off Campo Santo Stefano (Campo Francesco Morosini).

F6 Calle delle Botteghe, San Marco 3460 041 523 5310 Closed Tue San Samuele N, 2

HARRY'S BAR (€€€)

This legendary establishment is best known for its celebrity status (▷ panel). The restaurant upstairs serves reliable fare (although it can be very good, many say it is not what it used to be), while snacks can be ordered at the downstairs bar. This is the place to come for cocktails—the famous Bellini was invented here.

H7 Calle Vallaresso, San Marco 1323 041 528 5777 The bar is open every day but may close during carnival Vallaresso N, 1, 2

OSTERIA AL BACARETO (€€)

This well-placed traditional *trattoria* is in a quiet corner of the city just a few moments' walk west of the church of Santo Stefano. You can have a full meal, snack or a plate of antipasti with a glass of wine.

F6 Calle Crosera, San Marco 3447 041 528 9336 Closed Sat dinner, Sun Sant'Angelo or San Samuele N, 1, 2

PAOLIN (€–€€)

The best café in one of Venice's nicest squares. Lots of outside tables, and some of the city's best ice cream.

F6 Campo Santo

HARRY'S BAR

This famous bar and restaurant was founded in 1931 when, according to legend, a now-forgotten American ('Harry') remarked to hotel barman Giuseppe Cipriani that Venice lacked for nothing except a good bar. The enterprising Cipriani duly sought financial backing, found an old rope store near Piazza San Marco, and Harry's Bar was born. It is now a place of high prices, good food and great cocktails, and—in the words of writer Gore Vidal—'a babble of barbaric voices…the only place for Americans in acute distress to go for comfort and advice…'.

Stefano (Campo Francesco Morosini), San Marco 2962 041 522 5576 Closed Dec–Jan Accademia N, 1, 2

QUADRI (€–€€€)

www.quadrivenice.com
Not quite so famous or socially exalted as Florian (▷ 41), Quadri was abandoned by Venetian high society in the 19th century when it was frequented by officers of the occupying Austrian army. But prices reach Florian's stratospheric levels.

H6 Piazza San Marco, San Marco 120–4 041 522 2105 Closed Mon Vallaresso N, 1, 2

ROSA SALVA (€)

Venice's best café chain has outlets city wide. Coffees and cakes are good, but the atmosphere a bit sterile and bland.

H5 Campo San Luca, San Marco 4589 041 522 5382 Rialto N, 1, 2;
H6 Calle Fiubera, San Marco 5020 041 522 7934 Vallaresso 1, 2

ROSTICCERIA SAN BARTOLOMEO (€€)

A large self-service place that is good for snacks, especially at lunchtime. There is no cover charge or service downstairs (the restaurant upstairs has almost the same food but at a higher price). Near the Rialto, off Campo San Bartolomeo.

H5 Calle della Bissa, San Marco 5424 041 522 3569 Rialto N, 1, 2

Castello and Cannaregio are Venice's quietest and least-visited districts, peripheral —but still beautiful—areas where you can often escape the crowds. Castello is home to the great church of Santi Gionvanni e Paolo.

1

Canale delle Navi

2

Rio d'Sensa
Rio d'S Alvise
Campo d'S Alvise
Sant'Alvise
Convento
Rio di Zecchini
Ospedale Fatebenefratelli
Madonna dell'Orto
Rio Madonna dell'Orto
Palazzo Grimani Mayer
Fond d Cannaregio
Palazzo Michiel
Fond di Santa
Scuola dei Mercanti
C 80 Piave
C 80 Cavallo
Madonna dell'Orto
QUARTIERE GRIMANI
Casin degli Spiriti

S Girolamo
Rio di Sensa
Palazzo Mastelli
Palazzo Minelli Spada
Palazzo Contarini dal Zaffo

CANNAREGIO
IL GHETTO
Campo Ghetto Nuovo
Museo Ebraico
Fond di Misericordia
Campo dei Mori
Palazzo Longo
Casa Tintoretto
Rio di Mori

Palazzo Nani
Tempio Israelitico
Sacca della Misericordia

Palazzo Savorgnan
Parco di Savorgnan
Guglie
Ex Convento dei Servi di Maria
Cappella del Volto Santo
Palazzo Diedo
S Marziale
Palazzo Lezze
S Maria Valverde
Scuola Vecchia della Misericordia
Scuola Nuova della Misericordia
Ex Chiesa di Santa Caterina

Palazzo Venier
Rio Terra S Leonardo
Ex Scuola di San Leonardo
Ex Chiesa di Cristo
C 80 dell'Arcotetto
La Maddalena
Palazzo Correr Contarini
S Fosca
Palazzo Vendramin
Palazzo Molin
Palazzo Papafava
Rio di Racchetta
S Andrea

3

Canale di Cannaregio
Palazzo Labia
San Geremia e Lucia
PONTE DELLE GUGLIE
Palazzo Emo
San Marcuola
Palazzo Vendramin-Calergi (Casinò)
Palazzo Soranzo
Palazzo Emo
Palazzo Molin
Palazzo Gussoni-Grimani della Vida
Palazzo Boldù
S Felice
Campo S Felice
Palazzo Giovanelli
Rio di San Felice

Palazzo Flangini
Campo S Geremia
Palazzo Gritti
San Marcuola
Palazzo Zulian
Palazzo Barbarigo
Palazzo Fontana
S Sofia
Palazzo Sagredo
Santi Apostoli
Campo Santi Apostoli

San Marcuola

Canal Grande

Ca' d'Oro
Ca' d'Oro
Palazzo Foscari
Palazzo Michiel delle Colonne
Scuola dell'Angelo Custode
Ca' da Mosto
Palazzo Lion-Morosini
San Giovanni Crisostomo
Palazzo Corner
Palazzo Civran
S Sofia

4

5

Canal Grande

6

0   200 m
0   200 yds

E   **F**   **G**   **H**

Cimitero
San Michele

Isola di San Michele

Cimitero

Canale delle Fondamenta Nuove

Gesuiti
Palazzo Donà
Fondamente Nove
Oratorio dei Crociferi
Palazzo Zen
Campo dei Gesuiti
Ex Convento
Palazzo Seriman

San Lazzaro dei Mendicanti

Ospedale

Palazzo Widman

Campo San Canzian
San Canzian

Ospedale Civile

Santa Maria del Pianto

Palazzo Bembo e Boldù

Santa Maria dei Miracoli
Palazzo Sanudo
Monumento a Bartolomeo Colleoni
Campo Santi Giovanni e Paolo

Santi Giovanni e Paolo

Scuola Grande di San Marco

Teatro Malibran

Palazzo Pisani

Ospedaletto (Santa Maria dei Derelitti)

San Francesco della Vigna

Palazzo Gritti e della Nunziatora

Palazzo Cavagnis

Barbaria delle Tole

Ex Chiesa di S Giustina

Palazzo Contarini

Rio di San Marina

Giovanni Laterano

Ex Ospizio
Ex Lorenzo
San Lorenzo
Campo San Lorenzo

Palazzo Gradenigo

Palazzo Zorzi

Questura

Ex Convento

San Giovanni dei Cavalieri di Malta

Scuola di San Giorgio degli Schiavoni

Palazzo Priuli
Museo dei Dipinti Sacri Bizantini
San Giorgio degli Greci

S Antonino

San Martino

Palazzo Navagero

San Zaccaria
Convento

San Giovanni in Bragora

Riva degli Schiavoni
PONTE DEL VIN

Santa Maria della Visitazione o della Pietà

Ca' di Dio

Riva degli Schiavoni

Ex Forni

Arsenale

Canale di San Marco

J   K   L

3

4

Canale delle Fondamenta Nuove

San Francesco della Vigna

Celestia

Campo della Confraternita

5

Rio d'Celestia

Canale delle Galeazze

Palazzo Magno

Rio S Ternita

Darsena Arsenale Vecchio

Darsena Grande

Canale di Porta Nuova

Isola di San Pietro

Rio San Daniele

Arsenale

6

San Martino

Fond di Fronte

Campo Arsenale

Torri dell'Arsenale

Rio di San Pietro

Campo S Canise

Larisa S Pietro

Campo San Pietro

Ca' di Dio

Ex Forni

CASTELLO

Museo Storico Navale

Arsenale

Campo della

Rio della Tana

Fond della Tana

Palazzetto dello Sport

San Biagio

S Francesco di Paolo

Fond San Giacchino

Fond S'Anna

Ex Chiesa di S Anna

Rio di Quintavalle

7

Via Giuseppe Garibaldi

Monumento a Garibaldi

Fond San Giuseppe

C te Martin Novello

Canale di San Marco

Riva dei Sette Martiri

Giardini Garibaldi

Viale Garibaldi

Secco Marina

San Giuseppe di Castello

Rio d Quintavalle

8

Giardini Pubblici

Giardini

Biennale Internazionale d'Arte

Rio d Giardini

Via I Novembre

9

0 _____ 200 m

0 _____ 200 yds

L   **M**   **N**   **P**

The golden exterior may have faded but the Ca' d'Oro is a brilliant work of art

Ca' d'Oro

The smaller and less famous galleries of a city are often more rewarding. The Ca' d'Oro's collection of paintings, sculptures and objets d'art is one of the most absorbing in Venice.

Palace The Ca' d'Oro, or 'House of Gold', takes its name from the gilding that once covered its façade, a decorative veneer now worn away by wind and rain. The façade remains one of the most accomplished pieces of Venetian-Byzantine architecture in the city. The same, sadly, cannot be said of the interior, which has been ravaged by a succession of hapless owners. The palace was handed over to the state in 1916.

Exhibits The gallery divides into two floors, each of these arranged around a central *portego*. On the lower floor a captivating polyptych of the *Crucifixion* by Antonio Vivarini greets you, along with sculptural fragments belonging to the *Massacre of the Innocents* (14th century). Moving right you come to the gallery's pictorial masterpiece, Mantegna's sombre *St. Sebastian* (1506). To its left, in the *portego*, is a pair of busts by Tullio Lombardo (15th century), followed by six bronze reliefs, *The Story of the True Cross*, by Andrea Briscio (1470–1532). Rooms off the *portego* contain medallions, a *Madonna* by Giovanni Bellini and Florentine and Sienese paintings.

More art Upstairs there are tapestries, paintings by Titian, Van Dyck and Tintoretto, and damaged frescoes by Pordenone, Titian and Giorgione.

THE BASICS

www.cadoro.org
⊞ G4
⊠ Calle di Ca' d'Oro, Cannaregio 3932, off Strada Nova
☎ 041 520 0345
🕐 Mon 8.15–2, Tue–Sun 8.15–7.15
🚢 Ca' d'Oro N, 1
♿ Poor: stairs
💰 Moderate

HIGHLIGHTS

● Grand Canal façade
● *Massacre of the Innocents*, artist unknown
● *Crucifixion*, Antonio Vivarini
● *St. Sebastian*, Andrea Mantegna
● *Man and Woman*, busts by Tullio Lombardo
● *The Story of the True Cross*, bronze reliefs by Andrea Briscio
● *Madonna*, Giovanni Bellini
● *Flagellation*, Luca Signorelli

Madonna dell'Orto

TOP 25

The highly decorative exterior of Madonna dell'Orto and its magnificent interior art

THE BASICS

🔢 G2

✉ Campo Madonna dell'Orto, Cannaregio 3520

☎ 041 275 0494 or 041 275 0462

🕐 Mon–Sat 10–5, Sun 1–5

🚤 Orto 41, 42, 51, 52

♿ Good

💶 Inexpensive

❓ Chorus Pass (▷ 4)

HIGHLIGHTS

● Façade
● Doorway
● *St. Christopher*, Nicolò di Giovanni
● Campanile
● *St. John the Baptist*, Cima da Conegliano
● *Presentation of the Virgin*, Tintoretto
● *The Making of the Golden Calf*, Tintoretto
● *Last Judgement*, Tintoretto
● *St. Agnes Raising Licinius*, Tintoretto (Cappella Contarini)

Madonna dell'Orto ranks high among the many superb Venetian churches; its lovely setting well off the tourist trail and graceful redbrick façade are complemented by an airy interior filled with appealing works of art.

Exterior The first church on the present site was founded in 1350 and dedicated to St. Christopher, a statue of whom still dominates the lovely brick and marble façade. The building was rededicated to the Virgin in 1377, an act that was inspired by a miracle-working statue of the Madonna found in a nearby vegetable garden (*orto*). The elegant doorway, by Bartolomeo Bon, is a Renaissance-tinged work. Note the onion dome of the campanile, clear witness to the Byzantine influence on Venetian architecture.

Interior grandeur The artistic highlights begin above the first altar on the right, which has Cima da Conegliano's *St. John the Baptist* (1493). At the end of the right nave, above the door, stands Tintoretto's dramatic *Presentation of the Virgin* (1551). In the chapel to the right of the choir lies Tintoretto's tomb, together with those of his children, Domenico and Marietta. A wall separates the artist from two of his finest paintings, the choir's grand *Last Judgment* and *The Making of the Golden Calf*. Of the three paintings in the apse to the rear, those on the right and left—the *Beheading of St. Paul* and *St. Peter's Vision of the Cross*—are by Tintoretto; the central *Annunciation* is by Palma il Giovane.

Inside the church (left); Vivaldi's baptismal font (middle) and a record of his birth (right)

TOP 25

San Giovanni in Bragora

Choosing a preferred small Venetian church is no easy matter as there are so many contenders, but many have a soft spot for San Giovanni in Bragora, the baptismal church of the Venetian composer Antonio Vivaldi.

Names Founded in the 8th century, San Giovanni in Bragora is one of Venice's oldest churches, its name deriving possibly from *brágora*, meaning 'market-place'; or from two dialect words, brago ('mud') and *gora* ('stagnant canal'); or from the Greek agora, meaning 'town square'; from *bragolare* ('to fish'); or from the region in the Middle East that yielded the relics of St. John the Baptist, to whom the church is dedicated. The Venetian composer Antonio Vivaldi was baptised here, and the original font, together with copies of his baptismal documents, are in the left nave.

Works of art The paintings in the lovely interior begin on the south wall to the left of the first chapel with a triptych by Francesco Bissolo and a *Madonna and Saints* by Bartolomeo Vivarini. Between these, above the confessional, stands a small Byzantine Madonna. A relief above the sacristy door is flanked on the left by Alvise Vivarini's *Risen Christ* (1498) and by Cima da Conegliano's *Constantine and St. Helena* (1502). Cima also painted the church's pictorial highlight, *The Baptism of Christ* (1494). On the wall of the left aisle is a small *Head of the Saviour* by Alvise Vivarini and Bartolomeo Vivarini's *Madonna and Child* (1478), to the right of the second chapel.

THE BASICS

L6
Campo Bandiera e Moro, Castello 3790
041 520 5906
Mon–Sat 9–11, 3.30–5.30
Campo Bandiera e Moro
All services to San Zaccaria
Good
Free

HIGHLIGHTS

- Façade
- Vivaldi's baptismal font
- *Madonna and Saints*, Bartolomeo Vivarini
- Byzantine Madonna
- Relics of St. John the Almsgiver
- *Risen Christ*, Alvise Vivarini
- *Constantine and St. Helena*, Cima da Conegliano
- *The Baptism of Christ*, Cima da Conegliano
- *Head of the Saviour*, Alvise Vivarini
- *Madonna and Child*, Bartolomeo Vivarini

San Zaccaria

HIGHLIGHTS

- Façade bas-reliefs (1440), Antonio Gambello
- Upper façade, Mauro Coducci
- *Madonna and Child with Saints*, Giovanni Bellini
- Relics of San Zaccaria
- *The Birth of John the Baptist*, Tintoretto
- Crypt
- Vault frescoes, Andrea del Castagno
- Altarpieces, Antonio Vivarini and Giovanni d'Alemagna
- Predella, Paolo Veneziano

A charming medley of Gothic and Renaissance architecture whose calm interior contains Giovanni Bellini's *Madonna and Child with Saints*, one of Venice's most beautiful altarpieces.

Changes San Zaccaria was founded in the 9th century, received a Romanesque veneer a century later, and was overhauled again in 1174. Rebuilding began again in the 14th century, when the church acquired a Gothic look, though no sooner had it been completed than another new church was begun. Old and new versions are still visible, the brick façade of the earlier church on the right, the white marble front of the latter to its left. The newer façade is one of the most important in Venice, displaying a moment of architectural transition from Gothic to Renaissance. The Gothic lower

The restored Madonna and Saints by Giovanni Bellini (1505) in San Zaccaria (left); the façade of the church (middle top); detail of the carved ceiling (below left); a pollution damaged statue on the exterior of San Zaccaria (below right); the bell-tower of the church (right)

half is by Antonio Gambello, while the Renaissance upper section (added on Gambello's death in 1481) is the work of Mauro Coducci.

Who's who? The nave's second altar contains Giovanni Bellini's delightful *Madonna and Child with Saints* (1505). Across the nave in the second altar on the right lie the relics of San Zaccaria (Zachery or Zaccharias), the father of John the Baptist. The 'museum' off the south aisle has two linked chapels, the first of which contains an early Tintoretto, *The Birth of John the Baptist* (above the main altar). Steps in the adjoining Cappella di San Tarasio lead down to a 9th-century crypt, final resting place of eight of the city's first doges. The chapel's vaults contain early Renaissance frescoes (by Andrea del Castagno), while the altars below display three Gothic altarpieces by Antonio Vivarini.

THE BASICS

✚ K6
✉ Campo di San Zaccaria, Castello 4693
☎ 041 522 1257
🕐 Mon–Sat 10–12, 4–6, Sun 4–6
🍴 Campo San Provolo
🚢 All services to San Zaccaria
♿ Good
🎫 Church free. Cappella di San Tarasio inexpensive

Santa Maria dei Miracoli

The splendid church of Santa Maria dei Miracoli has some intricate paintings

THE BASICS

🟦 J4
✉ Campo dei Miracoli, Cannaregio 6075
☎ 041 275 0462
🕐 Mon–Sat 10–5, Sun 1–5
🍽 Campo Santa Maria Nova
🚤 Rialto N, 1, 2, 4
♿ Good
💰 Inexpensive
❓ Chorus Pass (▷ 4)

HIGHLIGHTS

● Tinted marbles
● Decorative inlays
● False pillars
● Bas-reliefs
● Nuns' choir
● Balustrade
● Pillar carving
● Raised choir
● *Madonna and Child*, Nicolò de Pietro
● Ceiling

You'll soon get used to being brought up short in Venice by surprises and views around almost every corner, but none quite compares with a first glimpse of the beautiful marbles of Santa Maria dei Miracoli.

Miracles The church was built to house an image of the Virgin, painted in 1409 and originally intended to be placed on the outside of a house (a common practice in Venice). Miracles (*miracoli*) began to be associated with the image in 1480, leading to a flood of votive donations that allowed the authorities to commission a church for the icon from Pietro Lombardo. One of the leading architects of his day, Lombardo created a building that relied for its effect almost entirely on shades, hues and tints, facing his church in a variety of honey-toned marbles, porphyry panels and serpentine inlays.

Interior grandeur Lombardo's innovative use of marble continues inside, which is filled with an array of sculptures that were executed in tandem with his sons, Tullio and Antonio. The best include the carving on the two pillars that support the nuns' choir (near the entrance); on the half-figures of the balustrade fronting the raised choir; among the exotica at the base of the choir's pillars. The striking ceiling portrays 50 *Saints and Prophets* (1528), by Pier Pennacchi. Nicolò di Pietro's *Madonna and Child*, the miraculous image for which the church was built, adorns the high altar.

The huge and impressive church of Santi Giovanni e Paolo (left) has a lofty nave (right)

Santi Giovanni e Paolo

Nowhere in Venice is there a greater collection of superb sculpture under one roof than in this majestic Gothic church whose walls are lined with the funerary monuments of more than 20 of the city's important doges.

Monuments Santi Giovanni e Paolo, known locally as San Zanipolo, is rivalled only by Santa Maria Gloriosa dei Frari (▷ 70–71). Its appeal rests on a handful of superb paintings, its tremendous tombs, and on surroundings that include the magnificent façade of the adjacent Scuola Grande di San Marco and Verrocchio's great equestrian statue of Bartolomeo Colleoni. The church was begun in 1246 by Doge Giacomo Tiepolo, who is buried in the most ornate of the four wall tombs built into the façade. Inside, further tombs lie around the walls, many by some of Venice's finest medieval sculptors. The best include the monuments to Doge Pietro Mocenigo (d1476) by Pietro, Tullio and Antonio Lombardo (left of the main door), and to Doge Michele Morosini (d1382), on the wall to the right of the high altar.

Paintings The most outstanding of the church's paintings are Giovanni Bellini's beautiful and recently restored polyptych of St. Vincent Ferrer (1464, second altar on the right) and the works in the south transept, which include *The Coronation of the Virgin*, attributed to Cima da Conegliano, and Lorenzo Lotto's wonderful *St. Antonius Pierozzi Giving Alms to the Poor* (1542).

THE BASICS

☒ J4

🖂 Campo Santi Giovanni e Paolo, Castello 6363

☎ 041 523 5913

🕐 Mon–Sat 9.30–6, Sun 1–6

🍴 Campo Santi Giovanni e Paolo

🚢 Fondamente Nuove or Ospedale 41, 42, 51, 52

♿ Good: one step

💲 Inexpensive

HIGHLIGHTS

● Main portal
● *Monument to Doge Pietro Mocenigo*, Pietro Lombardo
● *St. Vincent Ferrer*, Giovanni Bellini
● *St. Antonius Pierozzi Giving Alms to the Poor*, Lorenzo Lotto
● *Monument to Doge Michele Morosini*
● Veronese ceiling paintings, Cappella del Rosario
● Cappella della Madonna della Pace

Scuola di San Giorgio degli Schiavoni

HIGHLIGHTS

- St. George Slaying the Dragon
- Triumph of St. George
- St. George Baptising the Gentiles
- The Miracle of St. Tryphon
- The Agony in the Garden
- The Calling of St. Matthew
- The Vision of St. Augustine

TIP

- Allow time for your eyes to accustom to the dim light, and take time to pick out the detail in the paintings.

This intimate *scuola*, with its charming Carpaccio paintings, allows you the opportunity to look at works of art in the building for which they were painted, rather than in a gallery venue.

Slavs This tiny *scuola* (religious or charitable confraternity) was founded in 1451 to look after Venice's Dalmatian, or Slav (*Schiavoni*), population. Dalmatia, roughly present-day Croatia, was among the first territories absorbed by Venice (in the 9th century). In 1502 Carpaccio was commissioned to decorate their humble *scuola* with scenes from the lives of Dalmatia's three patron saints: George, Tryphon and Jerome. On their completion (in 1508), the paintings were installed in the headquarters' upper gallery and moved to their present position when the *scuola* was rebuilt in 1551.

Sitting in the grandeur of the Scuola di San Giorgio degli Schiavoni (far left); a magnificent ceiling in the scuola (top middle); stone fish detail (below left); St. George Slaying the Dragon by Carpaccio (below right); the façade of the scuola (right)

Art cycle Nine paintings, plus an altarpiece by Carpaccio's son, Benedetto, lie around the walls under one of the loveliest ceilings imaginable. The cycle starts on the north wall with *St. George Slaying the Dragon* (1502–08), a wonderfully graphic painting that is enlivened with a wealth of exotic and extraneous detail. Moving right you come to the *Triumph of St. George, St. George Baptising the Gentiles* and *The Miracle of St. Tryphon*, which depicts the obscure boy-saint exorcizing a demon from the daughter of the Roman Emperor Gordian. The next two, *The Agony in the Garden* and *The Calling of St. Matthew*, are followed by three works concerned with St. Jerome, an early father of the church: the best known is *The Vision of St. Augustine*, in which Augustine is visited by a vision announcing Jerome's death.

THE BASICS

➕ K5

✉ Calle dei Furlani, Castello 3259/a

☎ 041 522 8828

🕐 Mon 2.45–6, Tue–Sat 9–1, 2.45–6, Sun 9–1

🍴 Fondamenta di San Lorenzo

🚊 All services to San Zaccaria

♿ Good

👍 Moderate

More to See

ARSENALE

The Arsenale, Venice's vast former shipyards, are now used for exhibitions during Venice's *Biennale* and for the annual Festival of Boats each May. Work on opening more areas, more frequently, is ongoing.

✚ L6 ✉ Campiello della Malvasia, Castello ☎ 041 270 9546 🚇 41, 42, 71, 72 🖐 Varies with exhibition

CAMPO DEI MORI

This sleepy little square may take its name either from the Moorish merchants who traded on the *fondaco* nearby, or from three silk merchants—Robia, Sandi and Alfani Mastelli who settled in the Palazzo Mastelli north of the *campo*. In time they may have inspired the so-called Mori (Moors), three statues built into the walls of the piazza's houses. The building stands just east of the square at No. 3399 and was home to the painter Tintoretto between 1574 and his death in 1594.

✚ G2 ✉ Campo dei Mori, Cannaregio 🚇 Orto 41, 42, 51, 52

GESUITI

This large, dank church, built by the Jesuits in 1715, is renowned for its extraordinary marble *trompe-l'œil*, best seen in the pulpit on the left, whose solid stone is carved to resemble pelmets, tassels and curtains. The church also boasts Titian's *Martyrdom of St. Lawrence* (first chapel on the left) and Tintoretto's Assumption of the Virgin (left transept).

✚ J3 ✉ Campo dei Gesuiti, Cannaregio ☎ 041 528 6579 🕐 Daily 10–12, 4–6/7 ♿ Good 🖐 Free 🚇 Fondamente Nuove 41, 42, 51, 52

IL GHETTO

The Venetian ghetto lies in a fascinating area half-hidden in a corner of Cannaregio, enclosed by canals. The city's Jewish population were forced to live here until 1527. The district, which gave its name to all similar enclaves, most likely took its name from the foundries where cannons were cast (*gettare* means to cast). The area is still one rich in Jewish culture and history, including a monument to the

On guard outside the Arsenale

Moor statue in the Campo dei Mori

city's Jews murdered during the Holocaust, synagogues and the Jewish museum, the Museo Ebraico.

🅴 E2 **Museum:** ✉ Campo Ghetto Nuovo, Cannaregio 2902 ☎ 041 715 359, www.museoebraico.it 🕐 Sun– Fri 10–6 (7 in summer) 💶 Moderate 🚤 Guglie 41, 42, 51, 52 or San Marcuola N, 1, 2

ISOLA DI SAN MICHELE

It's a short hop on the *vaporetto* to Venice's wonderfully atmospheric cemetery island. Most of Isola di San Michele is covered by the cemetery, where Venetians are buried in tiers of stone coffin drawers or rest under an assortment of monuments.

🅴 L1–L2 ✉ Isola di San Michele ☎ 041 729 2811 🕐 Apr–end Sep daily 7.30–6; Oct–end Mar daily 7.30–4; 25 Dec, 1 Jan 7.30–12 💶 Free 🚤 Cimitero

MUSEO STORICO NAVALE

If you expected a dull and perfunctory museum, the Museo Storico Navale is a revelation. Its enjoyably presented displays of maritime ephemera put Venice and the sea into a clear historical context. There is a wonderful collection of gondolas and old boats in the separate Padiglione delle Navi.

🅴 M7 ✉ Campo San Biagio, Castello 2148 ☎ 041 520 0276 🕐 Mon–Fri 8.45–1.30, Sat 8.45–1 🚤 Arsenale 1, 41, 42 ♿ Poor 💶 Inexpensive

RIVA DEGLI SCHIAVONI

This broad quayside with its procession of *palazzi*, historic hotels, stalls and cafés, has great views, and is an ideal place for an evening stroll.

🅴 K6–L6 ✉ Riva degli Schiavoni, San Marco to Castello 🚤 All services to San Zaccaria

SAN FRANCESCO DELLA VIGNA

San Francesco takes its name from a vineyard left to the Franciscans here in 1253. Many alterations have been made since, not least the façade, built by Palladio between 1562 and 1572. The best painting is Antonio da Negroponte's *Madonna and Child* (1450) in the right transept.

🅴 L5 ✉ Campo San Francesco, Castello 2786 ☎ 041 520 6102 🕐 Daily 8–12, 3–7 🚤 Celestia 41, 42, 51, 52 ♿ Good 💶 Free

Floral tributes on the Isola di San Michele

Sublime art at San Francesco della Vigna

From the Ghetto to Piazza San Marco

A walk from the old Jewish Quarter in Cannaregio, down through Castello, passing some of the best churches in the city.

DISTANCE: 3km (2 miles) **ALLOW:** 3–4 hours with sights

START

CAMPO NUOVO, GHETTO
🔲 F2 🚏 Guglie 41, 42, 51, 52

1 Take Calle Farnese from Campo Ghetto Nuovo to Rio Terrà Farsetti. Turn left and then right on Fondamenta dei Ormesini. Take the second left, Calle del Forno.

2 Follow through to Fondamenta Madonna dell'Orto and the church (▷ 48) of the same name. From the church walk south through Campo dei Mori (▷ 56).

3 At Fondamenta della Misericordia, turn left and follow it to Calle della Rachetta. Then turn left and second right on Fondamenta Caterina.

4 Follow on to the Gesuiti (▷ 56), then walk south on Salizzada Seriman. Turn second right on Calle Vernier and follow through to Campeliello die Pietà.

END

RIVA DEGLI SCHIAVONI
🔲 K6 🚌 All services to San Zaccaria

8 Here you will find Santa Maria Formosa (▷ 32). Take Ruga Guiffa, then second left on Calle del Mezzo and Borgoloco San Lorenzo. Turn right on Fondamenta San Lorenzo to see San Giorgio degli Schiavoni and San Giorgio degli Greci. Walk south to Riva degli Schiavoni (▷ 57).

7 Turn right on Calle Larga Giacinto Gallina to visit Santi Giovanni e Paolo (▷ 53). From the church follow Calle del Ponte delle Erbe. Take the second left, Fondamenta Von Axel, to Campo di Santa Marina. Take Calle Pindemonte and then Calle del Borgoloco.

6 Continue into Calle Bondi to San Canzian. Cross the bridge in the far left corner of Campo Santa Maria Nova to see Santa Maria Miracoli (▷ 52). Retrace your steps across the bridge.

5 Carry on to Calle della Volta. Turn right and follow Calle del Fumo.

Shopping

ANTICLEA ANTIQUARIATO

This beautiful little shop is a wonderful collection of antique Venetian beads and jewellery. The owner has spent a lifetime amassing her stock, the best of which is kept in countless small drawers around the walls. Beads of your choice can be made up on the spot into earrings or necklaces.

K6 ✉ Campo San Provolo, Castello 4719a ☎ 041 528 6946 🚤 San Zaccaria 1, 2, 41, 42, 51, 52

BALLARIN

This excellent *pasticceria* has a superb range of cakes and pastries, to sample with a cup of coffee or takeout. It also makes delicious chocolates and sweets—look out for the chocolate-coated orange peel, candied fruit and fresh cream chocolate truffles.

H4 ✉ Salizzada San Giovanni Crisostomo, Cannaregio 5794 ☎ 041 528 5273 🚤 Rialto N, 1, 2

BARBIERI ARABESQUE

This elegant shop sells nothing but scarves, stoles and pashminas in silk, wool, cashmere and a great range of hues and styles; all tracked down by the English-speaking owner, who has excellent contacts in the silk-weaving towns around Lake Garda. Scarves for dressing up, keeping you warm and adding individuality and luxury to any outfit.

K6 ✉ Ponte dei Greci, Castello 3403 ☎ 041 522 8177 🚤 San Zaccaria 1, 2, 41, 42, 5, 52

CANTINA AD CANTON

This is a no-frills wineshop, where refills start at €1.90 per litre for something quite drinkable, such as Merlot, Tocai or Pinot Grigio. The location means cheaper prices, with a good bottle of *prosecco* for around €4.

F2 ✉ Fondamenta degli Ormesini, Cannaregio 2678 ☎ 041 713 129 🚤 Madonna dell'Orto 41, 42, 51, 52

CO-OP

If you are catering to yourself, or just want to pick up picnic supplies or

DEPARTMENT STORE

The only large department store worthy of the name is the excellent COIN, which sells a wide range of fashion, toiletries, accessories, china, linen, gifts and general goods. The staff win the prize for being among the most engaging shop assistants in Venice. It occupies a large corner block on the east side of Salizzada San Giovanni Crisostomo 5790 between the Rialto and the church of San Giovanni Crisostomo (🔲 H4). Visit Coin Beauty at Campo Santa Luca for endless beauty bargains.

a drink, it may be easier to head for a supermarket rather than struggle with non-English speakers in a traditional *alimentari* (general food store). There are two branches in Santa Croce; in Campo San Giaccomo dell'Orio and Fondamenta Santa Chiara (Piazzale Roma).

N7 ✉ Calle del Pistor, Castello 5989 ☎ 041 522 3415 🚤 Aresenale 1, 41, 42

GIANNI BASSO

Going into Gianni Basso's *stampatore* will take you back in time. The huge old printing presses are still in action, making business cards for people all over the world. Gianni has resisted change—he doesn't have a fax or website and takes orders by mail only. He also sells beautiful lithographs of Venice then and now.

J2 ✉ Calle del Fumo, Cannaregio 5306 ☎ 041 523 4681 🚤 Fondamente Nuove 1, N, 13, 25, 41, 42, 51, 52

JESURUM

www.jesurum.it
Factory-made (and often foreign-manufactured) lace has undercut and largely supplanted the famous traditional handmade specialty from Burano (▷ 106). As a result, original and old-style lace is now extremely rare and expensive. These two shops, near the Rialto bridge and Piazza San Marco, have an excellent selection of

both types, plus a fine collection of superb linens and lingerie. Other little shops selling lace, often at high prices, are dotted around the city. Place-settings and similar small pieces make excellent gifts.

➕ F2 ✉ Fondamenta della Sensa, Cannaregio 3219 ☎ 041 524 2540 🚤 Rialto N, 1, 2, 4

MISTERO

Mistero has two shops next to one another: one sells items for the home, another sells ladies' clothes (including a range of bigger sizes). The ladies' shop—Atelier—has amazing tops, all types of trousers, dresses and scarves imported from India, with a huge selection of styles to choose from.

➕ J6 ✉ Ruga Giuffa, Castello 4755 ☎ 041 522 7797 🚤 San Zaccaria N, 1, 2, 52, LN

MORI & BOZZI

It's worth a visit to this friendly shop down the Strada Nova if you like your shoe styles a little different from the norm—and cutting edge at that. There are many unusual shapes by trendy names, and budget shoppers can take their pick of designer copies.

➕ G3 ✉ Rio Terrà Maddalena, Cannaregio 2367 ☎ 041 715 261 🚤 San Marcuola N, 1, 2

LA NAVE D'ORO

Wine bars often sell wine by the bottle to take away and La Nave d'Oro outlets are typical. The wine is good and inexpensive, and embraces most of the Veneto's varieties, including some that are very hard to find elsewhere.

➕ J5 ✉ Calle del Mondo Nuovo, Castello 5786/b 🚤 Rialto N, 1, 2, 4

➕ F3 ✉ Rio Terrà San Leonardo, Cannaregio 1370 🚤 San Marcuola N, 1, 2

PANIFICIO VOLPE

Panificio Volpe specializes in traditional unleavened Jewish bread, pastries and confections, in a city not particularly renowned for its bread. This is one of the few really good Venetian bakeries. Get there early.

➕ E2 ✉ Calle del Ghetto Vecchio, Cannaregio 1143 ☎ 041 715 178 🚤 Guglie 41, 42, 51, 52

VIA GARIBALDI MARKET

This small but atmospheric market, just outside the north gates of the Via Garibaldi (gardens), sells fish, *salumeria* (cooked and cured meats), fruit and vegetables. If you are visiting the Museo Storico Navale or the Biennale, it is worth taking a look and enjoying a relatively tourist-free experience; if you're buying, prices are among the city's lowest.

🕐 Mon–Sat 8–1

PAULY

Pauly has been selling the finest Venetian glass since 1866. Its warren of showrooms contain all manner of treasures. There is also a big outlet on the Piazza San Marco.

➕ G3 ✉ Ponte Consorz Calle Largo, Castello 4391 ☎ 041 520 9899 🚤 All services to San Zaccaria

ROSA SALVA

This is a great place for those who need to stop for a sugar rush. Rosa Salva sells a huge range of cakes, chocolates and sweets; some for on-the-spot consumption and some to take home. The staff are very friendly, many Venetians rate their coffee the best in town, and prices are very reasonable at the bar.

➕ J4 ✉ Campo Santi Giovanni e Paolo, Castello 6779 ☎ 041 522 7949 🚤 Ospedale 25, 41, 42, 51, 52

VINO … E VINI

If you are unsure which kind of wines you should be taking home, ask the staff at Vino … e Vini. You'll get a detailed response and will come out of the shop with enough knowledge to impress your friends back home. You can also fill up plastic bottles here and buy gourmet specialties.

➕ L6 ✉ Fondamenta di Furlani, Castello 3301 ☎ 041 521 0184 🚤 San Zaccaria, Arsenale

Entertainment and Nightlife

ALGIUBAGIO

www.algiubagio.net
Right by the *vaporetto* landing stage, this busy, modern and welcoming bar is a good place for a warming or reviving drink waiting for, or after disembarking a boat. Or drop by during a stroll around the farther reaches of Cannaregio.
🔲 J3 ✉ Fondamente Nuove, Cannaregio 5039 ☎ 041 523 6084 🕐 Wed–Mon 7am–midnight 🚢 Fondamente Nuove 41, 42, 51, 52

CASINÒ MUNICIPALE DI VENEZIA

www.casinovenezia.it
Venice's popular Casinò Municipale (Municipal Casino), one of only a handful in Italy, is housed in the impressive Palazzo Vendramin-Calergi. Dress code is smart—a jacket and tie for men.
🔲 F3 ✉ Palazzo Vendramin-Calergi, Calle Larga Vendramin, off Rio Terrà della Maddalena, Cannaregio 2040 ☎ 041 529 7111 🕐 Daily 2.45pm–2.30am 🚢 San Marcuola N, 1, 2 💰 Expensive

CINEMA MULTISALA GIORGIONE MOVIE

A good selection of art-house films is shown at this two-screen Cannaregio cinema. Hollywood films are often dubbed into Italian.
🔲 H4 ✉ Rio Terrà dei Franceschi, Cannaregio 4612 ☎ 041 522 6298 🕐 Phone for latest details 🚢 Ca' d'Oro N, 1

ENOTECA ACIUGHETA

While the established Aciugheta restaurant and pizzeria is traditional in its look and approach, this co-owned *enoteca* (wine bar) alongside is an appealingly chic and contemporary space. You can eat full meals here, but this is more a place for a glass of wine and perhaps some *cicheti* (tapas-style snacks).
🔲 J3 ✉ Fondamente Nuove, Cannaregio 5039 ☎ 041 522 4292 🕐 Thu–Tue 7am–midnight 🚢 41, 42, 51, 52 and other services to Fondamente Nuove

FONDAZIONE QUERINI STAMPALIA

www.querinistampalia.it
This cultural institution organizes a diverse

WHAT'S ON

Details of films, concerts and exhibitions in Venice are listed in the '*Spettacoli*' section of daily editions of local newspapers such as *Il Gazzettino* and *La Nuova Venezia*. *Un Ospite di Venezia*, a free Italian/English magazine available from hotels and tourist offices, also contains detailed listings (published weekly in peak season, monthly during off-season). Tourist offices always have plenty of posters and leaflets on current events. Also keep an eye open for posters on the streets.

selection of artistic events, with regular Friday and Saturday classical concerts held in the opulent surroundings of a 15th-century *palazzo salone*.
🔲 J5 ✉ Campiello Querini Stampalia, Castello 5252 ☎ 041 271 1411 🕐 Hours vary 🚢 Rialto N, 1, 2 and all services to San Zaccaria

GIORGIONE

Venetians flock to this *trattoria*-cum-pizzeria for the quality food, Friulian wines and Venetian folk music. The owner, Lucio Bisutto, is one of the art's leading exponents and frequently performs his all-singing and a little dancing 'fisherman's tales from the *osterie*'.
🔲 M7 ✉ Via Giuseppe Garibaldi, Castello 1533 ☎ 041 522 8727 🕐 Closed Wed 🚢 Giardini N, 1, 41, 42, 51, 52, 61, 62

IGUANA

This Mexican bar and restaurant draws a crowd seeking sangria and song. Happy hour is from 6 to 7.30pm, but it's best to come later when the staff have warmed up a bit. Excellent burritos and fajitas, too.
🔲 G2 ✉ Fondamenta della Misericordia, Cannaregio 2515 ☎ 041 713 561 🕐 Tue–Sun 6pm–2am 🚢 Madonna dell'Orto 41, 42, 51, 52

INISHARK

Inishark serves Guinness and shows soccer on a wide-screen TV. Owners

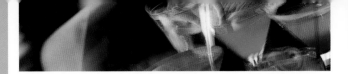

Alberto and Maria extend a warm welcome and are consistently entertaining.
F3 ✉ Calle del Mondo Novo, Castello 5787 ☎ 041 523 5300 🕑 Tue–Sun 6pm–1.30am 🚢 Rialto N, 1, 2

LA CANTINA
There are a number of bars on the Strada Nova but this is by far the best. It serves beer *alla spina* (on tap) and wines, and is a good place to pop into if you're passing.
G3 ✉ Campo San Felice, Cannaregio 3689 ☎ 041 522 8258 🕑 Mon–Sat 11–11 🚢 Ca' d'Oro N, 1

PARADISO PERDUTO
The atmosphere at this renowned nightspot makes up for the fairly average food that is served here. The inexpensive wine and eclectic music attract a diverse, alternative crowd, and its legendary all-night theme parties have ruffled many locals' feathers over the years.
G2 ✉ Fondamenta della Misericordia, Cannaregio 2640 ☎ 041 720 581 🕑 Tue–Sun 11–3, 6–2 🚢 Madonna dell'Orto 41, 42, 51, 52

TEATRO FONDAMENTE NUOVE
Venice's premier avant-garde venue, wonderfully set on the northern lagoon in remote Cannaregio, was founded in 1993 in an old joiners' shop. It stages contemporary dance and organizes performances,

film festivals, workshops and exhibitions as part of its innovative Art and Technology project, which explores the relationship between artistic creativity and technology.
J3 ✉ Fondamente Nuove, Cannaregio 5013 ☎ 041 522 4498 🕑 Phone for latest details 🚢 Fondamente Nuove 1, N, 13, 25, 41, 42, 51, 52

TEATRO MALIBRAN
A theatre has stood on this site since 1677, and the Teatro Malibran was Venice's most élite performance venue throughout the 18th century. It stages well-known operas such as *La Traviata* and more modern works, as well as classical concerts and first-class ballet productions.
H4 ✉ Calle dei Milion, Cannaregio 5873 ☎ 041 786 603; box office 041 786 601 🕑 Phone for latest details 🚢 Rialto N, 1, 2

WHERE TO GO
Nightlife in Venice is decidely low key. Late-night possiblilities are really limited to bars and live-music cafés, where you can hear jazz, blues or reggae, with the occasional Latino or rock session. A main party area is Fondementa della Misericordia in Cannaregio, where a string of waterfront bars and tiny clubs transforms the whole quayside into one long nightspot.

TEATRO PICCOLO ARSENALE
Since 2002 the organization responsible for the *Biennale*, Venice's two-yearly international arts show, has started to turn former buildings of the Arsenale into exhibition and performance spaces such as the Teatro Piccolo and Piccolo Arsenale.
M6–N6 ✉ Arsenale ☎ 041 523 5300 🕑 Contact tourist information for details or www.labiennale.org 🚢 Arsenale 1, 41, 42

UN MONDO DI VINO
Charming owners and a warm atmosphere make this tiny wine bar a great place to join a throng of locals for an inexpensive glass of wine and snacks. Located immediately west of Campo Santa Maria Nova a few steps from the lovely church of Santa Maria dei Miracoli.
J4 ✉ Salizzada San Canzian (or San Canciano), Cannaregio 5984/b ☎ 041 521 1093 🕑 Tue–Sun 10–3, 5.30–9.30 🚢 Rialto N, 1, 2

ZENEVIA
This bar is popular for its intimate nooks inside and its seating outside on Campo Santa Maria Formosa. Giant spritz and Guinness are consumed by an up-for-it crowd. Occasional live music.
J5 ✉ Campo Santa Maria Formosa, Cannaregio 5548 ☎ 041 520 6266 🕑 Wed–Mon 9pm–2am 🚢 Zattere, Rialto

Restaurants

PRICES

Prices are approximate, based on a 3-course meal for one person.
€€€   over €55
€€   €35–€55
€   under €35

AI PROMESSI SPOSI (€)

This friendly bar-restaurant serves up fish dishes that are both inexpensive and come in huge portions. The tasty bar snacks are also excellent and even less expensive.

➕ H4 ✉ Calle dell'Oca, Cannaregio 4367 ☎ 041 522 8609 🅞 Daily 🚤 Ca' d'Oro N, 1

AI TREI SPIEDI (€)

Tricky to find but worth it. A spot that's popular with locals but not always discovered by visitors. It's inexpensive, and serves some honest-to-goodness Venetian cuisine.

➕ H4 ✉ Salizzada San Canzian, Cannaregio 5906 ☎ 041 520 8035 🅞 Closed Sun lunch, Mon 🚤 Rialto N, 1, 2

AL COVO (€€€)

Charming two-room restaurant in a calm, romantic and tasteful setting. It is usually possible to eat out in the adjacent little square in summer. The service is generally warm and polite—the owner's wife at front of house is American—while the highly accomplished

cooking focuses on traditional Venetian recipes using the best ingredients. Fish dishes predominate the regularly changing menu (when there is one), servings are small, the cooking fresh and refined and the wine list is good. With only 50 seats, be sure to reserve ahead.

➕ L6 ✉ Campiello della Pescaria, Castello 3968 ☎ 041 522 3812 🅞 Closed Wed, Thu, and 2 weeks in Aug and Jan 🚤 Arsenale 1, 41, 42

ALLA RIVETTA (€)

An inexpensive but good trattoria close to Piazza San Marco that makes a pleasant alternative to some of the more expensive places. Small and often very busy.

➕ J6 ✉ Ponte San Provolo, near Campo SS Filippo e

THE COST

The bill (check; il conto) usually includes a cover charge per person (pane e coperto) and a 10–15 per cent service charge (servizio). Restaurants are required by law to give you a proper receipt (una ricevuta). Always look at your bill carefully, especially if—as still happens—it is an illegible scrawl on a piece of paper (strictly speaking illegal). Skipping antipasti and desserts will reduce costs—go to a gelateria for an ice-cream instead.

Giacomo, Castello 4625 ☎ 041 528 7302 🅞 Closed Mon and Aug 🚤 All services to San Zaccaria

AL MASCARON (€€)

A nice bar-trattoria with a brisk, informal atmosphere, a beamed ceiling and a line of old black-and-white photos on the walls. Venetian fish and seafood cooking is served at the brown, heavy wood tables on paper tablecloths. So popular—reservations are essential—that the owners have opened the similar Alla Mascareta for wine and snacks a few doors down the same street at No. 5183.

➕ J5 ✉ Calle Lunga Santa Maria Formosa, Castello 5525 ☎ 041 522 5995 or 041 523 0744 🅞 Closed Sun and mid-Dec to mid-Jan 🚤 Rialto N, 1, 2

BOLDRIN (€)

Excellent and spacious enoteca in the northern part of the city. Wine by the glass and hot snacks. Wonderfully mixed clientele—old ladies with little dogs to paint-spattered builders.

➕ J4 ✉ Salizzada San Canzian (or San Canciano), Cannaregio 5550 ☎ 041 523 7859 🅞 Closed Sun 🚤 Rialto N, 1, 4, 2

CORTE SCONTA (€€)

Many Venetians and visitors alike rate the Corte Sconta as their preferred among the city's restaurants, despite its slightly

peripheral location (close to the Arsenale). Fairly small and always busy, and the cooking and seafood are rarely less than excellent. No menu as such, so try to follow waiting staff's recommendations. A small garden is open for outdoor eating in summer. Somewhat hard to find.

➕ L6 ✉ Calle del Pestrin, Castello 3886 ☎ 041 522 7024 🕐 Closed Sun, Mon 🚢 Arsenale 1, 41, 42

DA REMIGIO (€€)

Small area *trattorie* are a dying breed in Venice, so this authentic restaurant, despite a redecoration that has removed some old-fashioned touches, is a find. It has just 40 seats, so reserve or arrive early to share a table. The food is reliable and homey, and although the wine list is short it is adequate.

➕ K6 ✉ Salizzada dei Greci, Castello 3416 ☎ 041 523 0089 🕐 Closed Mon dinner and Tue 🚢 Arsenale 1, 41, 42 or all services to San Zaccaria

FIASCHETTERIA TOSCANA (€€)

Despite the 'Toscana' in its name, the menu at this beloved restaurant established in 1956 includes classic Venetian dishes and seafood.

➕ H4 ✉ Salizzada San Giovanni Cristostomo, Cannaregio 5719 ☎ 041 528 5281 🕐 Closed Tue, lunch Wed and a period in Jul 🚢 Rialto N, 1, 2, 4

OSTERIA ALLE TESTIERE (€€)

www.osterialletestiere.it
One of the top tables in town, if you can get a reservation. The food is cheap given the quality that cooking a limited menu for small numbers allows the owner to achieve. The focus is on local dishes but imaginatively prepared and full of zinging tastes.

➕ J5 ✉ Calle del Mondo Novo, Castello 5801 ☎ 041 522 7220 🕐 Mon–Sat, seatings at 7 and 9.15pm 🚢 Rialto N, 1, 2

OSTERIA OLIVA NERA (€€€)

www.osteria-olivanera.com
One of a new breed challenging the old school of Venetian restaurateurs. Its mostly fish and seafood menu shows Venetian cooking can be given a

---

MORE OPTIONS

Fixed-price tourist menus (*menù turistico*) usually include a basic pasta, main course, fruit and half-bottles of wine and water. Food quality is often indifferent—you will probably find many of the same dishes listed on the menu in a budget *trattoria* as in most expensive restaurants. The difference is primarily one of ambience and detail. The *prezzo fisso* menu usually excludes cover, service and beverages. Check what is included in the price.

---

contemporary edge. All fish is fresh from the market. A second restaurant, Oliva Nera II, has opened in the same street at 3447 (closed Thu) offering a more meat-based menu while retaining the same priniciples of fresh home cooking.

➕ K6 ✉ Salizzada dei Greci, Castello 3417–18 ☎ 041 522 2170 🕐 Thu–Tue 12–2.30, 7–10 🚢 All services to San Zaccaria

LA TERRAZZA (€€€)

Venice's trendy hotels all have fine restaurants and the Danieli is no exception. Refined Venetian and international cooking is served with panache on the stylish terrace overlooking the Grand Canal. Fine service and an excellent wine list, all at high prices.

➕ J6 ✉ Riva degli Schiavoni-Calle delle Rasse, Castello 4196 ☎ 041 522 6480 🚢 All services to San Zaccaria

VINI DA GIGIO (€€)

A pretty, relaxed and romantic restaurant on a peaceful canal: just two simple rooms with beams and old wooden cabinets. Venetian cooking including fish and meat dishes, and a short, well-chosen wine list. Good for lunch or dinner.

➕ G3 ✉ Fondamenta della Chiesa-San Felice, Cannaregio 3628a ☎ 041 528 5140 🕐 Closed Sun dinner, Mon, Jan and 3 weeks in Aug 🚢 Ca' d'Oro N, 1

While visitors flock to see the top sights in this area, few venture to the many quieter corners of San Polo and Santa Croce. This makes their maze of squares and alleys some of the best in the city to explore.

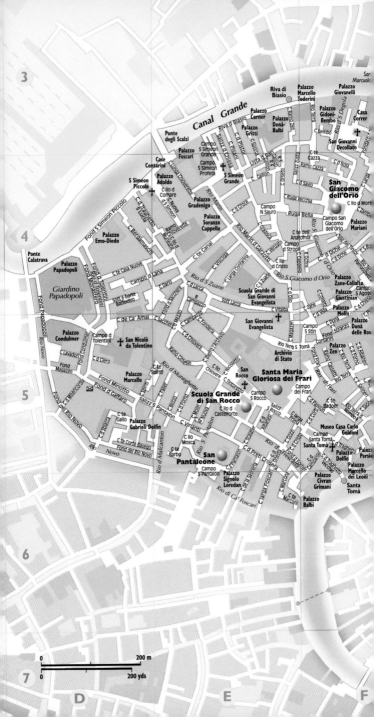

3

Canal Grande

Riva di Biasio

Palazzo Marcello Toderini

Palazzo Giovanelli

San Marcuola

Palazzo Corner

Palazzo Gritti

Palazzo Donà-Balbi

Palazzo Gidoni-Bembo

Casa Correr

Ponte degli Scalzi

Palazzo Foscari

Campo S Simeón Grande

Riva di Biasio

San Giovanni Decollato

Case Contarini

Campo S Simeón Profeta

S Simeón Grande

San Giacomo dell'Orio

S Siméon Piccolo

Palazzo Adoldo

S Simeón Piccolo

4

Palazzo Gradenigo

Campo N Sauro

Campo San Giacomo dell'Orio

Palazzo Mariani

Palazzo Soranzo Cappello

Campo dell'Anatomia

Campo di Strope

Palazzo Emo-Diedo

Ponte Calatrava

Palazzo Zane-Collalto

Palazzo Papadopoli

Campo d'Lana

Rio d S Zuane

Larga contarina

Campo S Agostin

Palazzo Giustinian

Giardino Papadopoli

Scuola Grande di San Giovanni Evangelista

Palazzo Molin

San Giovanni Evangelista

Palazzo Donà delle Ros

Palazzo Zen

Palazzo Condulmer

San Nicolò da Tolentino

Campo S Stin

Campo S Tomà

Rio Terra S Tomà

Archivio di Stato

Palazzo Marcello

San Rocco

Santa Maria Gloriosa dei Frari

5

Scuola Grande di San Rocco

Campo S Rocco

Campo dei Frari

Palazzo Gabrieli Dolfin

Museo Casa Carlo Goldoni

Campo Santa Tomà

Santa Tomà

Palazzo Dolfin

Palazzo Persie

San Pantaleone

Campo S Pantalon

Palazzo Sigolo Loredan

Palazzo Marcello dei Leoni

Santa Tomà

Palazzo Civran Grimani

Rio di Ca' Foscari

Palazzo Balbi

6

7

0 ————— 200 m

0 ————— 200 yds

D　　　　　　**E**　　　　　　**F**

Canal Grande

Fondaco dei Turchi
Palazzo Belloni Battagia
Ca' Tron
Palazzo Priuli-Bon
San Stae
Museo di Storia Naturale
Palazzo Priuli-Stazio
San Stae
Campo S Stae
Palazzo Foscarini-Giovanelli
Museo del Tessuto e del Costume
Palazzo Corner della Regina
Ca' Pesaro
Palazzo Donà
Casa Favretto
Palazzo Mocenigo
Santa Maria Mater Domini
Palazzo Zane
S Maria Mater Domini
Campo
Palazzo Agnus Dio
Palazzo Brandolin
S Sofia
Fontamenta Nuova
Palazzo Grioni
Palazzo Moro
San Cassiano
Palazzo Gozzi
Campo S Cassiano
Pescheria
Campo d Pescaria
Fabbriche Nuove
Palazzo Muti-Baglioni
Fabbriche Vecchie
Palazzo Bernardo
Palazzo Albrizzi
C.llo Albrizzi
Palazzo Molin-Cappella
Campo S Beccarie
San Giovanni Elemosinario
Gobbo di Rialto
Mercato Rialto
S Giacomo d Rialto
Sant'Aponal
Campo S Aponal
Erberia
Campo Rialto Nuovo
Palazzo Dieci Savi
SAN POLO
Palazzo Corner Mocenigo
Palazzo Soranzo
Campo San Polo
Palazzo Maffetti Tiepolo
Campo S Silvestro
Ponte di Rialto
San Polo
Palazzo Barzizza
San Silvestro
Palazzo Ravà
Palazzo orner
Palazzo Donà della Madonnetta
Palazzo Grimani
Palazzo Donà
Palazzo Papadopoli
San Silvestro
Canal Grande
Riva di Vin
Palazzo sani-oretta
Palazzo Barbarigo
Palazzo Cappello-Layard
Palazzo Bernardo
Palazzo Tiepolo
Santa Tomà

G   H

Canal Grande

TOP 25

TIPS

● The *vaporetto* is probably
the best way of seeing the
canal; gondolas and taxis are
far more expensive.
● If time is short take the
No. 2, which has fewer stops
than the No. 1.

**The world's most beautiful 'street'
offers an endlessly unfolding pageant
with superb views of the city's finest
palaces and a fascinating insight into
Venetian life.**

A riot of life and noise Snaking 4km (2.5 miles)
through the heart of Venice, it divides the city:
Three of the city's six districts, or *sestieri*, lie to one
side and three to the other. At most hours of the
day and night it is alive with boats and bustle,
providing an almost hypnotic spectacle when
admired from one of its three bridges (the Scalzi,
Rialto and Accademia) or from the heavily laden
vaporetti that ply up and down its length. In
addition to the life of the canal is the attraction of
the palaces that line its banks, an historical digest
of the city's most appealing architecture dating

The Rialto Bridge over the Canal Grande by night (top left); vaporetti and gondolas ply the canal (top right); looking across to the Bacino di San Marco from the Canal Grande (below left); by night from the Accademia Bridge (below middle left); travel in style by gondola (below middle right); more views along the canal (below right)

back over 500 years. From the Ponte di Rialto, Venice's most famous bridge, you get a view of the canal at it's most franatically busy.

Jump on board A trip along this intriguing canal is a pleasure in itself, and one that you can never tire of. Board either vaporetto No. 1 or No. 2 at Piazzale Roma or the Ferrovia (rail station), making sure the boat is heading in the right direction. For the best views, try to secure one of the few outside seats at the front or rear of the boat: Venetians prefer to stand in the middle. The Rialto and Accademia bridges make convenient breaks in the ride, but for your first trip stay aboard all the way to San Marco (and then do the return trip to take in the glory of the palaces on the opposite bank). It is also well worth making the trip at night, when the experience, if anything, is even more magical.

THE BASICS

✚ D4–G7

🚏 1, 2 (year-round)

♿ Good

💰 Moderate

❓ *Vaporetto* 1 halts at every stop; 2 stops at Piazzale Roma, Ferrovia, San Marcuola, Rialto, Sant'Angelo, San Tomà, San Samuele, Accademia and Vallaresso

Santa Maria Gloriosa dei Frari

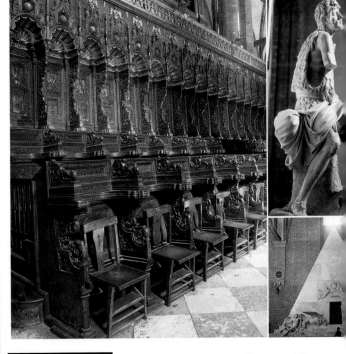

HIGHLIGHTS

- *Madonna and Child*, Giovanni Bellini
- *Assumption*, Titian
- *Madonna di Ca' Pesaro*, Titian
- *Madonna and Child* (1339), Paolo Veneziano (sacristy)
- *St. John the Baptist*, Donatello
- *Mausoleo Tiziano* (Tomb of Titian)
- Wooden choir (124 stalls)
- *Monumento al Doge Giovanni Pesaro*
- *Monumento al Canova*

If you were allowed to walk away with just one work of art from Venice it could well be Bellini's sublime altarpiece in this church, the largest and most important of the city's churches.

Magnificent edifice The Frari narrowly outranks Santi Giovanni e Paolo in size and importance. Founded around 1250, it became the mother church of the city's Franciscans, after whom it is named—*frari* is a Venetian corruption of *frati*, meaning 'friars'.

The greats interred Many of the city's great and good are buried in the church, among them the painter Titian (*d*1576), whose 19th-century tomb occupies the second altar on the right (south) wall. Opposite, on the left wall, stands the *Monumento*

al Canova (1827), an unmistakable marble pyramid that contains the sculptor's heart. The composer Claudio Monteverdi (*d*1643) is buried in the third chapel to the left of the high altar.

Art The Frari's most striking painting is Titian's *Assumption* (1516–18), its position above the high altar designed to attract your attention from most of the church. Look at the same painter's influential *Madonna di Ca' Pesaro* (1526), on the last altar of the left aisle. The most beautiful work of art in the church, however, is Giovanni Bellini's sublime triptych of the *Madonna and Child between Sts. Nicholas, Peter, Mark and Benedict* (1488), located in the sacristy off the right transept. In the first chapel on the right of the high altar is Donatello's statue of *St. John the Baptist* (1438), the only work in Venice by the famous Florentine sculptor.

THE BASICS

🗺 E5

✉ Campo dei Frari 3072, San Polo 3072

☎ 041 275 0462 or 041 275 0494

🕐 Mon–Sat 9–6, Sun 1–6

🍴 Campo dei Frari

🚊 San Tomà N, 1, 2

♿ Good: one or two steps

💷 Inexpensive

❓ Chorus Pass (▷ 4)

Scuola Grande di San Rocco

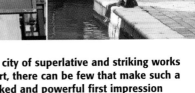

HIGHLIGHTS

● *Crucifixion*
● *Moses Strikes Water from the Rock*
● *The Fall of Manna*
● *The Temptation of Christ*
● *The Adoration of the Shepherds*
● Wooden sculptures
● *The Flight into Egypt*
● *Annunciation*

TIPS

● Allow 1 to 2 hours for a thorough visit.
● Start your visit upstairs in the Albergo.

In a city of superlative and striking works of art, there can be few that make such a marked and powerful first impression than the colossal cycle of 54 paintings by Tintoretto that line the walls here.

From rags to riches This *scuola*, formerly a charitable institution for the sick, was founded in 1478 in praise of St. Roch, a saint whose efficacy against disease made him popular in pestilence-ridden Venice. In 1564, having become one of the city's wealthiest fraternities, the *scuola* instigated a competition to decorate the walls of its hall. It was won by Tintoretto, who then spent some 23 years creating one of Europe's greatest painting cycles.

The wonders inside To see Tintoretto's 54 paintings in the order they were painted, ignore

The sublime interior of the Chapter House (top left); the exterior of the scuola (top right); the sign of the scuola (below left); houses on the canal behind the scuola (below middle left); the 16th-century Scuola Grande with a smaller 18th-century building alongside (below middle right); Crucifixion (1565) by Tintoretto (below right)

the canvases on the ground level and in the main hall (Sala Grande) up the stairs. Instead, go to the Sala dell'Albergo (off the main hall), dominated by a huge *Crucifixion* (1565), often described as one of Italy's greatest paintings. The room's central ceiling panel is *St. Roch in Glory*, the painting that won Tintoretto his commission. In the main hall are ceiling paintings (1575–81) describing episodes from the Old Testament, all carefully chosen to draw parallels with the *scuola's* charitable or curative aims. The 10 wall paintings show scenes from the New Testament. Note the superb 17th-century wooden carvings around the walls, by the little-known sculptor Francesco Pianta. Of the eight paintings downstairs, the artist's last in the *scuola* (1583–88), the best are the idiosyncratic *Annunciation* and *The Flight into Egypt*.

THE BASICS

www.scuolagrande
sanrocco.it

🔢 E5

✉ Campo San Rocco, San Polo 3052

☎ 041 523 4864

🕐 Apr–end Oct daily 9–5.30; Nov–end Mar daily 10–5

🍴 Campo dei Frari

🚤 San Tomà N, 1, 2

♿ Poor

💷 Expensive

❓ A leaflet about the *scuola's* paintings is usually free with your ticket

More to See

CA' PESARO

www.museiciviveneziani.it

The Ca' Pesaro presents its best face to the Grand Canal, but its waterfront façade can also be glimpsed from the ends of several alleys off the Strada Nova. It was bought as three separate buildings in 1628 by the Pesaro family, who subsequently commissioned Baldassare Longhena, one of Venice's leading 17th-century architects, to unite the component parts behind one of the city's grandest baroque façades. Today it houses Venice's Galleria d'Arte, Galleria Internazionale d'Arte Moderna (Gallery of Modern Art) and the Museo d'Arte Orientale displaying Chinese and Japanese art and objects.

🔲 G4 ⊠ Canal Grande-Fondamenta Ca' Pesaro, Santa Croce 2070–76 ☎ 041 721 127 🕐 Galleria and Museo Apr–Oct Tue–Sun 10–6; Nov–Mar Tue–Sun 10–5 🚏 San Stae N, 1 ♿ Poor ✋ Galleria and Museo moderate

MERCATO RIALTO

The Rialto has it all, whether you want to shop for souvenirs, people-watch or revel in the sights and smells of a market. Early in the morning, before the crowds arrive, is the best time for a stroll around the fantastic medley of food (*erberia*) and fish stalls (*pescheria*).

🔲 H4–H5 ⊠ Rialto 🚏 Rialto N, 1, 2

MUSEO DI STORIA NATURALE

www.museiciviveneziani.it

Venice's Natural History Museum is housed in the old Fondaco dei Turchi, the Turks' Warehouse. In 1922 it became the home of a small natural history collection. Downstairs there's an aquarium containing species that live in the Adriatic and some information on the ecology of the lagoon. Due to restoration work, only parts of the museum can be currently visited.

🔲 F3 ⊠ Fondaco dei Turchi, Santa Croce 1730 ☎ 041 275 0206 🕐 Tue–Fri 9–1, Sat, Sun 10–4 ✋ Free 🚏 San Stae N, 1

PALAZZO MOCENIGO

www.museiciviveneziani.it

The Palazzo Mocenigo near San Stae is one of several *palazzi* in the city built by the Mocenigo family, one of

Tempting vegetables on sale in the Mercato Rialto

Ca' Pesaro, a vision of Venetian baroque architecture

the grandest and oldest of the noble Venetian clans. The palace now houses the Museo del Tessuto e Costume and is worth a visit for a fascinating glimpse of the style in which the 18th-century nobility lived.
➕ F4 ✉ Salizzada San Stae, Santa Croce 1992 ☎ 041 721 798 🕓 Closed for restoration work and due to reopen early 2009 🚤 San Stae N, 1

SAN GIACOMO DELL'ORIO

Few Venetian buildings feel as old as San Giacomo, founded in the 9th century and added to over the years to produce an architectural hybrid. The 14th-century Gothic ship's-keel ceiling and the wooden Tuscan statue of the *Madonna and Child* are wonderful. There are magnificient paintings in the old and new sacristies and a high altarpiece, *Madonna and Child,* by Lorenzo Lotto.
➕ F4 ✉ Campo San Giacomo dell'Orio, Santa Croce 1456 ☎ 041 275 0462 🕓 Mon–Sat 10–5, Sun 1–5 🚤 Riva di Biasio or San Stae 1 🦽 Good 💵 Inexpensive ❓ Chorus Pass (▷ 4)

SAN PANTALEONE

San Pantaleone is best known for its gargantuan ceiling painting, Gian Antonio Fumiani's *The Miracles and Martyrdom of St. Pantaleone* (1704). Smaller paintings include Veronese's touching piece *St. Pantaleone Healing a Boy* (1587; second chapel on the right).
➕ E5 ✉ Campo San Pantalon, San Polo 3765 ☎ 041 523 5893 🕓 Mon–Sat 8–10, 4–6 🚤 San Tomà 1, 2 🦽 Good 💵 Free

SAN POLO

Founded in 837 but much altered since, the church of San Polo is renowned for Giandomenico Tiepolo's *Via Crucis*, or *Stations of the Cross* (1747), an 18-panel cycle of paintings in the sacristy. Tintoretto's turbulent *Last Supper* (1547) hangs on the west wall, while the apse chapel contains Veronese's *Marriage of the Virgin*.
➕ F5 ✉ Campo San Polo, San Polo 2102 ☎ 041 523 7631 or 041 275 0462 🕓 Mon–Sat 10–5, Sun 1–5 🚤 San Silvestro 1 🦽 Good 💵 Inexpensive ❓ Chorus Pass (▷ 4)

The striking Fondaco dei Turchi, home to the Museo di Storia Naturale

Shopping

ALIANI GASTRONOMIA
Perhaps Venice's most famous delicatessen, this shop has a superlative selection of cheeses, together with a variety of hams, salamis, fresh pasta and other ready-made delicacies.
✚ G5 ✉ Ruga Vecchia San Giovanni, San Polo 654 ☎ 041 522 4913 🚤 Rialto or San Silvestro N, 1, 2

BALOCOLOC
www.balocoloc.com
All the hats sold here are original and handmade by the owner, Silvana Martin, who changes her designs to suit the season. There are lovely brimmed hats, doge like knitted hats in bright designs and some pretty berets. You can take your time and have a real rummage while Silvana sits making up her creations in the background. The shop also stocks costumes for the *Carnevale* at better prices than some of the more well-known shops. There is a second outlet in Cannaregio at Strada Nova 326.
✚ G4 ✉ Calle Longa, Santa Croce 2134 ☎ 041 524 0551 or 041 640 273 🚤 San Silvestro N, 1, 2

LA CANTINA
Even though it's more expensive than other wine shops in the outlying areas, you can get your empty bottles refilled from €2.50 per litre of red wine. A bottle of *prosecco* costs around €5.
✚ G5 ✉ Ruga Rialto (also known as Ruga Vecchio San Giovanni), San Polo 970A ☎ 041 523 5042 🚤 San Silvestro 1

CASA DEL PARMIGIANO
www.aliani-casadelparmigiano.it
A stone's throw from the main Rialto markets, this little family-run shop sells superb cheese, *salumeria* (delicatessen) from all over Italy and light-as-a-feather homemade fresh pasta. Locals consider this one of the best shops in Venice, so be prepared to stand in line. A number of cheeses and salamis are vacuum-packed, ideal for taking home.
✚ H5 ✉ Erberia, San Polo 214–15 ☎ 041 520 6525 🚤 Rialto N, 1, 2

THE RIALTO

As a district the Rialto is almost as old as the city itself, the earliest settlers having been attracted to its high banks, or *rivo alto*, these forming a dry and easily defended redoubt amid the marsh and mud of the lagoon. While San Marco developed into the city's political heart, the Rivoaltus became its commercial hub, where all manner of staple and exotic goods were traded in the 'Bazaar of Europe'.

COLORCASA
This shop is crammed with some of the most sumptuous decorating fabrics you can imagine—silks, brocades and figured velvets are for sale by the length or made up into cushions, drapes and bags. Silk key tassels and curtain swags are equally tempting, and ColorCasa stocks wonderfully warm *trapunti* (quilted bed-covers) in vivid fabrics.
✚ F5 ✉ Campo San Polo, San Polo 1989–91 ☎ 041 523 6071 🚤 San Tomà N, 1, 2

DROGHERIA MASCARI
www.imascari.com
On the 'street of spice merchants' near the Pescheria (fish market), this wonderful shop, crammed with interesting foods, spices, dried fruit and nuts, teas, coffees and sweets, also has nicely wrapped packets of dried mushrooms, jars of truffles, balsamic vinegar and beautiful biscuits. It's a great place for that take-home foodie souvenir, such as a jar of Frank Cooper's Oxford marmalade.
✚ G4 ✉ Ruga dei Spezieri, San Polo 382 ☎ 041 522 9762 🚤 Rialto or San Silvestro N, 1, 2

EMILIO CECCATO
If there is one souvenir, over and above glass, that greets you at every turn in Venice, it is the fake and mass-produced gon-

dolier's straw hat. This unique little shop sells the genuine article, together with gondoliers' garb—hats, tunics and trousers—to both gondoliers and curious foreigners.

 H5  Sottoportego di Rialto, San Polo 1617 ☎ 041 522 2700  Rialto N, 1, 2, 4

ERBERIA

Venice's main outdoor market provides a wonderful spectacle of sound and vibrancy, its stalls laden with fruit and vegetables, its thoroughfares busy with shoppers and traders. Explore the maze of stalls north of Campo San Giacomo di Rialto, not merely the more touristy stalls that line the Ruga degli Orefici.

 H5  Campo San Giacomo di Rialto  Rialto N, 1, 2, 4

GILBERTO PENZO

What more appropriate gift or souvenir to take home from Venice than a gondola? This shop sells beautiful handmade wooden models of the boats, as well as gondola prints, posters and simple models (perfect for children) either as kits or ready-made and painted.

 F5  Calle Il Saoneri, San Polo 2681 ☎ 041 719 372  San Tomà N, 1, 2

HIBISCUS

A rainbow of hot Indian hues shines in the great selection of ethnically inspired scarves, jackets, bags and jewellery in this

tempting store, a wonderful, if expensive, contrast to the vast number of cheap glass and mask shops in this area. The clothes are well cut and comfortable, and the stock changes continually.

 G5  Ruga Rialto, San Polo 1060–61 ☎ 041 520 8989  San Silvestro 1

LEGATORIA POLLIERO

This tiny, old-fashioned shop alongside Santa Maria Gloriosa dei Frari, offers a lovely selection of leather-bound and marbled paper stationery, together with handmade gifts and beautiful individual sheets of paper.

 F5  Campo dei Frari, San Polo 2995 ☎ 041 528 5130  San Tomà N, 1, 2

MERCATO DI RIALTO

Traders have been selling

PRACTICALITIES

Food shops and bakeries are usually open 8.30–1 and 4–7, though virtually all close on Wednesday afternoon and Sunday. For locals, mornings are set aside for food shopping and this is the time to visit the city's markets at the Rialto and the locality, which open around 8.30. Food served by weight (including bread) is sold by the *chilo*, *mezzo chilo* (kilo and half-kilo: about 2lb and 1lb) and, more commonly, by the *etto* (100g: about 4oz), plural *etti*.

their fruit, vegetables and other produce here for 1,000 years. While much is shipped from the mainland, the tone, plumpness and taste of the goods is still far superior to what we're used to in supermarkets back home. Look out for the truly local produce from Sant'Erasmo, labelled 'San Rasmo' or *'nostranni'*. Only open in the mornings Monday to Saturday.

 H4–H5  Ruga degli Orefici, San Polo  Rialto N, 1, 2

PESCHERIA

Venice's evocative fish market, its stalls loaded with all manner of exotic-looking fish and seafood, merges seamlessly with the fruit and vegetable stalls of the adjoining Erberia. Mornings only Tuesday to Saturday.

 G4–H4  Campo della Pescaria, Fondamenta dell'Olio, San Polo  Rialto N, 1, 2

TRAGICOMICA

www.tragicomica.it
Superb handmade masks, created by an artist trained at Venice's Accademia delle Belle Arti, echo the 18th-century heyday of *Carnevale*. Look out for Harlequins, Columbines and pantaloons, the plague doctor and some imaginative mythological masks.

 F5  Calle dei Nomboli, San Polo 2800 ☎ 041 721 102  San Tomà N, 1, 2

Entertainment and Nightlife

ANTICO DOLO

The Rialto market district has a great many old-fashioned wine bars, and this is one of the best. Good lunchtime snacks (the tripe is famous) and a small but fine menu for evening meals.

✚ G5 ✉ Ruga Vecchia San Giovanni, San Polo 778 ☎ 041 522 6546 🕐 Daily 12–10/11pm 🚤 Rialto N, 1, 2

ARENA DI CAMPO SAN POLO

For six weeks from late July to early September this large *campo* is transformed into an open-air cinema, attracting audiences of up to 1,000 people. The backdrop of flickering hues across crumbling Venetian buildings adds to the drama. Films are usually dubbed into Italian.

✚ F5 ✉ Campo San Polo, San Polo ☎ 041 524 1320 🕐 Phone for latest details 🚤 San Silvestro 1, San Tomà N, 1, 2

BAGOLO

Located on a pretty and tucked-away square with small cafés, bars and restaurants. Bagolo is an atmospheric place to drink, particularly with its low lighting and candlelit tables out on the *campo* in summer.

✚ F4 ✉ Campo San Giacomo dell'Olio, Santa Croce 1584 ☎ 041 717 584 🕐 Tue–Sun 8–2 🚤 Riva de Biasio 1, 51, 52

CAFFÉ DEI FRARI

This is a great place for an aperitif, especially if you want to dine nearby. Many Venetians start their night with the house spritz or a glass of *prosecco*.

✚ F5 ✉ Fondamenta dei Frari, San Polo 2564 ☎ 041 524 1877 🕐 Daily 8am–9pm. Closed 15 days in Aug 🚤 San Tomà N, 1, 2

CHIESA DI SAN GIACOMETTO

www.prgroup.it
This intimate church of San Giacomo di Rialto, affectionately known as San Giacometto, near the Rialto markets is considered by many to be the oldest in Venice. Frequent concerts by the Ensemble Antonio Vivaldi and other guest orchestras.

✚ H4 ✉ Campo di San Giacometto, San Polo ☎ 041 426 6559 🕐 Phone or visit website 🚤 Rialto, San Silvestro 1

EVENING PASTIMES

Venice does not have the nightlife to match other major cities. For many Venetians an evening out consists of a meal or drink with friends rounded off with a stroll to a bar for a coffee or ice cream. One of the best places to join them is in squares such as Campo San Polo (✚ F5). *Scuole* and churches are also popular for classical music concerts.

DO MORI

The most authentic and atmospheric of Venice's old-time *bacari*, in business since 1462. Always filled with locals, shoppers and traders from the nearby Rialto markets. Good snacks; 350 wines. No seats or tables.

✚ G4 ✉ Calle do Mori, off Ruga Vecchia San Giovanni, San Polo 429 ☎ 041 522 5401 🕐 Mon–Sat 8.30–8.30 🚤 Rialto N, 1, 2

SACRO E PROFANO

The Sacred and Profane bar has the kind of name that might put nervous visitors off, but it conceals a lively and very Venetian place near the Rialto Bridge that's tiny and always packed with a very vocal local crowd. Great atmosphere.

✚ H4 ✉ Ramo Terzo del Parangon, San Polo 502 ☎ 041 523 7924 🕐 Closed Wed 🚤 Rialto N, 1, 2

SANTA MARIA GLORIOSA DEI FRARI

www.chorusvenezia.org,
www.basilicadeifrari.it
There are regular sacred music concert series in spring and autumn, sometimes featuring orchestral ensembles, other times organ recitals. A great setting for music.

✚ E5 ✉ Campo dei Frari, San Polo ☎ 041 522 2637 🕐 Phone for latest details 🚤 San Tomà N, 1, 2

Restaurants

PRICES

Prices are approximate, based on a 3-course meal for one person.

€€€ over €55
€€ €35–€55
€ under €35

ALLA MADONNA (€€)

One of Venice's most authentic restaurants, and one of the oldest in the city—it has the look of a Venetian restaurant of 30 years ago. A popular preference for business meetings and family celebrations. The good food is rigorously Venetian, including such typical dishes as *sarde in saôr*, *zuppa di pesce* and *ai frutte di mare*.

H5 ✉ Calle della Madonna, San Polo 594 ☎ 041 522 3824 ◉ Closed Wed and 2 weeks in Aug 🚤 Rialto N, 1, 2

ALLE NONO RISORTE (€–€€)

You can have full meals here, but most of the locals go for pizza. Service can be a bit hit or miss, but in summer, while relaxing in the wisteria-draped canal-side garden, any annoyances are easy to shrug off. Hidden away off the alley between Campo San Cassiano and Calle della Regina.

G4 ✉ Sotoportego de Siora Bettina, Santa Croce 2338 ☎ 041 524 1169 ◉ Closed Wed, Thu lunch 🚤 San Stae N, 1

ALLE OCHE (€–€€)

Just south of the quiet little square of Campo San Giacomo dell'Orio. This restaurant is very popular, so reserve or arrive early to secure a table outside, and enjoy one of the many pizzas.

F4 ✉ Calle del Tintor, San Polo 1552 ☎ 041 524 1161 🚤 Riva di Biasio 1

ANTICA BIRRARIA LA CORTE (€€€)

This converted warehouse is one of a new breed of Venetian restaurants. The seating spills out into the evocative expanse of Campo San Polo, making

DRINKS

Venice's water is perfectly safe to drink, though Venetians prefer mineral water (*acqua minerale*)—either sparkling (*gassata*) or still (*liscia, naturale* or *non gassata*). Bottles come in one litre (*un litro* or *una bottiglia*) or half-litre (*mezzo litro* or *mezza bottiglia*) sizes. Bottled fruit juice is *un succo di frutta*, available in pear (*pera*), apricot (*albiccoca*), peach (*pesca*) and other tastes. Fresh juice is *una spremuta*, while milk shake is *un frullato*, or *un frappé* if made with ice cream. Lemon soda is a popular and refreshing bitter-lemon drink. Ice is *ghiaccio*, and a slice of lemon is *uno spicchio di limone*.

it perfect for sunny days and balmy evenings. The inside is contemporary, with clean lines and chrome predominating. The food nods to all the Venetian and Italian classics—it's good quality and won't break the bank. You can snack or go the whole hog here.

F5 ✉ Campo San Polo, San Polo 2168 ☎ 041 275 0570 ◉ Tue–Sun 11–3, 6–10 🚤 San Silvestro 1

CIAK (€)

Pleasant and relaxed bar after visiting Santa Maria Gloriosa dei Frari and the Scuola Grande di San Rocco. Used by everyone from gondoliers to society ladies. Good lunchtime snacks and sandwiches.

F5 ✉ Campo San Tomà, San Polo 2807 ☎ 041 528 5150 🚤 San Tomà N, 1, 2

DA FIORE (€€€)

This small, highly acclaimed restaurant produces excellent Venetian cuisine, which is conjured up by its self-taught owners. Since it was named as one of the 'world's best' restaurants, it has become extremely difficult to get a table. Hard to find.

F4 ✉ Calle del Scaleter, San Polo 2002/a ☎ 041 721 308 ◉ Closed Sun, Mon and 3 weeks in Aug 🚤 San Stae or San Silvestro N, 1

DA IGNAZIO (€€)

This fairly small and predominantly fish restaurant

lies just east of Campo San Tomà, and has the atmosphere of a restaurant from the 1950s. Garden for alfresco dining in summer.

✠ F5 ✉ Calle Saoneri, San Polo 2749 ☎ 041 523 4852 🛈 Closed Sat and 3 weeks in Jul and Aug 🚤 San Tomà N, 1, 2

NARANZARIA (€€)
www.naranzaria.it
Near the Rialto Bridge and the Market, this Venetian version of a tapas/sushi bar has tables by the canal and dining upstairs, too. There's a full menu ranging from prawn couscous with mint to local dishes, and a wide wine list. It's always busy—a good sign.

✠ H4 ✉ Campo San Giacometto, San Polo 130 ☎ 041 724 1035 🛈 Closed Mon 🚤 Rialto N, 1, 2

OSTERIA LA ZUCCA (€€)
The imaginative and ever-changing food here, especially the vegetable side dishes and main courses, are innovative, at least by Venice's normally conservative standards. Nice location.

✠ F4 ✉ Calle del Tintor (or Tentor), Santa Croce 1762 ☎ 041 524 1570 🛈 Closed Sun 🚤 Riva di Biasio 1, 51, 52

POSTE VECIE (€€€)
Ingredients could hardly be fresher than at this appealing fish restaurant

in an old mail house alongside the Rialto's Pescheria fish market. The cooking is refined, but can be variable, and there's a good wine list. Reputedly founded in 1500.

✠ H4 ✉ Campo della Pescaria, San Polo 1608 ☎ 041 721 822 🛈 Closed Tue and 4 weeks in Jul and Aug 🚤 Rialto N, 1, 2, 4

IL REFOLO (€)
Popular with locals for good pizzas and a limited selection of pastas and main courses. A nice position in a quiet corner close to the church.

✠ F4 ✉ Campo San Giacomo dell'Olio, Santa Croce 1459 ☎ 041 524 0016 🛈 Closed Mon, Tue lunch and Nov–Mar 🚤 Riva di Biasio or San Stae 1

ETIQUETTE
The procedure when standing up in a bar is to pay for what you want at the cash desk (la cassa) and take your receipt (lo scontrino) to the bar, where you repeat your order (a tip slapped down on the bar works wonders with the service). Do not then take your drink and sit at an outside table, as you almost always pay a premium to sit down when you order through a waiter. Sitting, a single purchase allows you to relax and watch the world go by almost indefinitely.

RIBÓ (€€€)
This is a refreshingly bright and modern restaurant, serving light and modern Venetian cuisine, and a little off the usual tourist trail. Expect reasonable (though not inexpensive) prices, superb fresh pasta and fresh fish, and a romantic interior patio garden

✠ D5 Fondamenta Minotto, Santa Croce 158 ☎ 041 524 2486 🛈 Closed Wed, 2 weeks in Aug 🚤 San Basilio N, 2, 61, 62

TRATTORIA SAN TOMÀ (€–€€)
Both the pizzas and trattoria food served here are good, but this restaurant's best attraction is its location on Campo San Tomà, only one minute south of Santa Maria Gloriosa dei Frari and the Scuola Grande di San Rocco.

✠ F5 ✉ Campo San Tomà, San Polo 2864 ☎ 041 523 8819 🛈 Closed Tue in winter 🚤 San Tomà N, 1, 2

VIVALDI (€–€€)
This small, relaxed and pleasantly Venetian place produces simple hot dishes that can either be eaten informally at the front or sitting down at a few tables to the rear, where more ambitious (and more expensive) meals are also available.

✠ G5 ✉ Calle della Madonnetta, San Polo 1457 ☎ 041 523 8185 🛈 Closed Sun 🚤 San Silvestro 1

Dorsoduro is the most distinctive of Venice's six *sestieri*, a curving narrow arm that embraces the southern reaches of the Grand Canal. Quiet and mostly residential, it is a pleasure to wander at random.

3

4

Canal Grande

5

Fond. dei Rio Novo

Fond. di S. Maria Maggiore · Fond. di S. Maria Mag. · Fond. le Procuratie
Rio di Tintor
Rio Terrà dei sacri
C.te Contarini
C.te Cerere
C.ta Nova

Santa Margherita

Campo Santa Margherita

Scuola dei Varotari

6

QUARTIERE SANTA MARTA

S Teresa

San Nicolò dei Mendicoli

Oratorio · Rio di San Nicolò

Palazzo Cicogna

Palazzo Foscarini

Istitutio Superiore d'Arte Applicata

Campo
C.te

Scuola Grande dei Carmini

San Barnaba

Fond. Barbarigo
Fond. di Peschiera

Angolo Raffaele

San Raffaele

Campo Angelo Raffaele

Collegio Armeno

Santa Maria dei Carmini

Campo dietro il Cimitero

Campo Zopee

San Sebastiano

STAZIONE MARITTIMA

Banchina di San Basilio

Palazzo Molin

San Basilio

DORSODURO

Ospedale G B Giustinian

Ognissanti

Fond. Ognissanti

Campo Ognissanti

STAZIONE MARITTIMA

Palazzo Brandoli

San Trovaso

Campo Trovaso

Squero di San Trovaso

Fond. Zattere al Ponte Lungo

Zattere

7

Canale di Fusina

Canale della Giudecca

8

9

0 ——— 200 m
0 ——— 200 yds

B   **C**   **D**   **E**

Canal Grande

Ca' Foscari
Palazzo Giustinian
Palazzo Nani

Ca' Rezzonico
Palazzo Contarini-Michiel
Ca' Rezzonico
San Samuele
alpaga Palazzo Stern
Palazzo Moro
Palazzo Loredan
Toleta Palazzo Contarini degli Scrigni
C.no
Malpiero
Accademia
Palazzo Querini
Campo Carità
Palazzo Contarini-Dal Zaffo

Ponte dell'Accademia

Palazzo Loredan
Palazzo Cini
Campo S Vio
Palazzo Da Mula

Collezione Peggy Guggenheim

Santa Maria del Giglio

Canal Grande

Palazzo Barbarigo
Palazzo Salviati
Palazzo Dario

Ex Abbazia di San Gregorio
Palazzo Genovese
Ex Chiesa di San Gregorio

Salute
Campo d Salute
Fond Dogana alla Salute

Punta della Dogana

Santa Maria della Salute
Seminario Patriarcale

Dogana di Mare

Palazzo Giustinian Recanati
Gallerie dell' Accademia
Palazzo Nani

S Maria d Visitazione
S Agnese
Campo S Agnese
Fond Zattere ai Gesuati
Gesuati
Zattere

Ex Convento

Ex Ospizio

Ospedale degli Incurabili
Fond Zattere allo Spirito Santo
Spirito Santo

Fond Zattere ai saloni

Isola della Giudecca

F G H

Ca' Rezzonico

Venetian furniture and paintings (left) on show in the Ca' Rezzonico museum (right)

THE BASICS

www.museicivicivenaziani.it

⊞ E6

✉ Fondamenta Rezzonico, Dorsoduro 3136

☎ 041 241 0100

🕓 Apr–end Oct Wed–Mon 10–6; Nov–end Mar Wed–Mon 10–5. Ticket office closes 1 hour earlier

🍴 Campo San Barnaba

🚤 Ca' Rezzonico 1

♿ Good

💷 Expensive

❓ Museum Pass (▷ 4)

Gazing at the Grand Canal's palaces from a boat you can't help but wish to see inside some of them, which is the attraction of Ca' Rezzonico, a museum that re-creates a Venetian palace as it might have been in the 18th century.

How it began The Ca' Rezzonico was begun in 1667 by Baldassarre Longhena, one of the leading architects of his day, but remained half-finished. In 1751 the shell was bought by the Rezzonico family and then passed through several hands before opening as a museum in 1936. It begins in fine style with a sumptuous ballroom done with *trompe-l'œil* and huge chandeliers. Highlights of rooms include ceiling frescoes by G. B. Tiepolo, some fine lacquerwork, Flemish tapestries and pastel portraits by Rosalba Carriera.

HIGHLIGHTS

● Ballroom
● G. B. Tiepolo ceiling frescoes
● Carriera portraits
● Lacquerwork
● Gondola cabin, or *felze*
● Canaletto paintings
● Francesco Guardi paintings
● Pietro Longhi paintings
● G. D. Tiepolo satirical frescoes

The collection Much of the palace is devoted to a picture gallery, whose highlight is a pair of paintings by Canaletto, two of only a handful that remain on public display in Venice. Also of interest are Francesco Guardi's views of the city's convents and gambling rooms, together with 34 amateurish but fascinating portraits of Venetian life by Pietro Longhi, among them his well-known *Rhinoceros*, painted during the animal's stay in Venice in 1779. Rooms off to the right include a splendid bedchamber, complete with 18th-century closet and sponge-bag. Of special note are a series of satirical frescoes (1793–97) by G. D. Tiepolo, a collection of traditional puppets, an old pharmacy and the fine views from the palace's upper floors.

Guggenheim statue
(left) and a view
down the Grand Canal
from the gallery (right)

Collezione Peggy Guggenheim

It's rather apt that the Accademia and Guggenheim, Venice's two most visited galleries, are so close together, juxtaposing two matchless collections of paintings and sculptures—one traditional and one modern.

Perfect setting The Guggenheim's small but polished collection was accumulated by Peggy Guggenheim (1898–1979), daughter of an American copper magnate, and installed by her in the 18th-century Palazzo Venier dei Leoni. The collection's appeal owes much to its immaculate presentation as well as to the beauty of its setting, many of the sculptures being arranged in a lovely garden. This has works by Henry Moore, Paolozzi, Giacometti and others, and houses the New Wing and appealing 'Museum Store'.

Modern art Guggenheim's taste and money allowed her to select high-quality works from virtually every modern-art movement of the 20th century. At the same time she had a penchant for the surreal and avant-garde, having enjoyed a brief relationship with the Surrealist painter Max Ernst. The collection features Cubist works by Picasso and Braque, and the Surrealism of Dalí, Magritte and Mirò. American modernists include Jackson Pollock and Rothko, while the English are represented by Francis Bacon. There are also sculptures by Calder and Brancusi, as well as works by Italian Futurists Balla and Boccioni. The most memorable work is Marino Marini's provocative *Angel of the Citadel*, on the terrace overlooking the Grand Canal.

THE BASICS

www.guggenheim-venice.it
🔲 G7
✉ Palazzo Venier dei Leoni, Calle San Cristoforo, Dorsoduro 704
☎ 041 240 5411
🕐 Wed–Mon 10–6
⛴ Salute 1
♿ Good
💷 Expensive

HIGHLIGHTS

● The New Wing
● Henry Moore sculptures
● *Bird in Space*, Constantin Brancusi
● *Red Tower*, De Chirico
● *Robing of the Bride*, Max Ernst
● Silver bedhead, Alexander Calder
● Jackson Pollock paintings
● *The Poet*, Pablo Picasso
● *Angel of the Citadel*, Marino Marini

DORSODURO

★

TOP 25

TOP
25

Gallerie dell'Accademia

HIGHLIGHTS

● *Madonna and Saints*, Giovanni Bellini (Room 2)
● *Tempest*, Giorgione (Room 5)
● *Supper in the House of Levi*, Veronese (Room 10)
● *The Translation of the Body of St. Mark*, Tintoretto (Room 10)
● *Pietà*, Titian (Room 10)
● Pietro Longhi paintings (Room 17)
● The Miracles of the True Cross' (Room 20)
● 'Life of St. Ursula', Carpaccio (Room 21)

Art awaits you at every turn in this city, but you would miss a key experience without a visit to the Accademia, home to the world's greatest collection of Venetian paintings.

Masterpieces The Accademia began life as Venice's art school in 1750, moving to its present site in 1807 when it garnered much of its permanent collection from churches and religious houses suppressed by Napoleonic decree. Its paintings, arranged chronologically, spread across 24 rooms. Some of the gallery's best-known paintings are found in the first five rooms, Room 1 opening with Byzantine works, a style that influenced the city's earliest painters. Rooms 2 to 5 contain canvases by Carpaccio, Mantegna, Bellini and others, reflecting Venice's Renaissance heyday, as well as

Madonna and Child *by Bellini (far left); waiting for opening time (top left); Room 24 with 15th-century paintings by Vivarini (top right); ceiling in Room 1 by Marco Cozzi (below left); paintings by Bellini and Girogione in the former church nave, now Room 23 (below middle); Room 10—paintings by Tintoretto and Veronese (below right)*

the Accademia's most famous painting, Giorgione's mysterious *Tempest* (c1500). Rooms 10 and 11 have High Renaissance masterpieces, such as Veronese's *Supper in the House of Levi* (1573) and Tintoretto's iconoclastic *Miracle of the Slave* and *The Translation of the Body of St. Mark* (c1560).

Cycles Leave plenty of time for the Accademia's highlights, two *storie*, or fresco cycles (Rooms 20 and 21). The first, 'The Miracles of the True Cross' (1494–1510), was painted by a variety of artists for the Scuola di San Giovanni Evangelista. Each describes a miracle worked by a relic of the 'True Cross' owned by the *scuola*, though often the miracle itself takes second place to the fascinating anecdotal detail. The same is true for the second cycle, painted by Carpaccio for the Scuola di Sant' Orsola, with episodes from the 'Life of St. Ursula'.

THE BASICS

www.gallerieaccademia.org

⊞ F7

✉ Campo della Carità, Dorsoduro 1050

☎ 041 522 2247

🕐 Tue–Sun 8.15–7.15, Mon 8.15–2

🍴 Campo Santo Stefano

🚏 Accademia N, 1, 2, 3, 4

♿ Poor: some steps

💰 Expensive

TIPS

● Try to avoid Sunday and arrive early if you can.

● English-language tours are available.

San Sebastiano

The interior of San Sebastiano is decorated with fine ceiling decoration and statues

THE BASICS

www.chorusvenezia.org
🔲 D7
✉ Campo San Sebastiano, Dorsoduro 1686
☎ 041 275 0462
🕐 Mon–Sat 10–5, Sun 1–5
🍴 Campo Santa Margherita and Campo San Barnaba
🚤 San Basilio N, 2, 61, 62
♿ Good
💷 Inexpensive
❓ Chorus Pass (▷ 4)

HIGHLIGHTS

● Sacristy
● Ceiling
● Choir and Nuns' choir
● Organ
● *St. Nicholas* (1563), Titian (first chapel on right)
● *Madonna and Child* (16th century), Tommaso Lombardo (second chapel on right)
● *Tomb of Archbishop Podocattaro of Cyprus* (d1555), Sansovino (fourth chapel on right)

While paintings by some of Venice's artists—notably Titian and Tintoretto—are often showcased in grandiose settings, the city's finest collection of works by Veronese is gathered in the humble little church of San Sebastiano.

Veronese Born in Verona, Paolo Caliari Veronese (1528–88) moved to Venice while he was in his twenties, settling close to San Sebastiano, which became his parish church. In 1555 he was commissioned to decorate the sacristy, where he left paintings of the *Evangelists* and the *Coronation of the Virgin*. Impressed by his work, the church authorities gave him free rein to decorate the ceiling. The three main panels depict episodes from the story of Esther, chosen for its symbolic parallels with the stories of Eve and the Virgin Mary.

Monopoly Veronese also painted the high altarpiece—the *Madonna and Child with Sts. Sebastian, Peter, Francis and Catherine* (1570)—and the two vast paintings on the north and south walls. The latter portray *Sts. Mark and Marcellinus Led to Martyrdom and Comforted by St. Sebastian* and *The Second Martyrdom of St. Sebastian* (Sebastian survived his first assault by arrows and was martyred by being pummelled to death). Veronese also painted *The Trial and Martyrdom of St. Sebastian* in the nuns' choir, above the church's west end. He even designed and painted the organ, his decorative monopoly of San Sebastiano making it only fitting that he was buried here: His tomb, and that of his brother, lie in front of the chapel.

Both inside and out, Santa Maria della Salute has some superb decoration

Santa Maria della Salute

In a city where almost every street and canal offers a memorable vista, this church, proudly situated at the entrance to the Grand Canal, forms part of the panorama most people commonly associate with Venice.

Plague In 1630 Venice found itself ravaged by a plague so severe that the Senate promised to build a church in celebration of the Virgin if she could save the city. Within weeks the pestilence had abated, and on 1 April the following year the first stone of the Salute, meaning 'health' and 'salvation' in Italian, was laid. Its architect was Baldassare Longhena. His design proved to be a baroque model for years to come, combining the Palladian influence of his master, Scamozzi (Palladio's closest follower), with a range of personal innovations.

Baroque interior The Salute's main impact is as a distant prospect, its dazzling exterior detail and great dome (fashioned on that of St. Peter's in Rome) forming irreplaceable elements of the Venetian skyline. The church's interior is more restrained, and its fine marble floor is the first thing that catches your eye. Moving left from the side entrance, the third of the three altars boasts an early painting by Titian, the *Descent of the Holy Spirit* (1550). The high altar supports *The Virgin Casting out the Plague* (1670), a magnificent sculpture designed by Longhena and carved by Juste le Court. The supplicant figure on the left represents Venice, while the elderly harridan moving off to the right symbolizes the plague.

THE BASICS

www.seminariovenezia.it

G7

Campo della Salute, Dorsoduro

041 522 5558

Daily 9–12, 3–5.30

Salute 1

Poor: several steps

Church free. Sacristy inexpensive

HIGHLIGHTS

● Marble floor
● *Descent of the Holy Spirit*, Titian
● *The Virgin Casting out the Plague*, Juste le Court
● *Feast at Cana* (1561), Tintoretto (sacristy)
● *Cain and Abel* (1542–44), Titian (sacristy)
● *David and Goliath* (1542–44), Titian (sacristy)
● *Sacrifice of Abraham* (1542–44), Titian (sacristy)
● *St. Mark Enthroned between Sts. Cosmas, Damian, Roch and Sebastian* (1510), Titian (sacristy)

Scuola Grande dei Carmini

Simple detail outside the scuola (left) and elaborate ceiling by S. Ricci inside (right)

THE BASICS

🔲 D6

✉ Campo dei Carmini, Campo Santa Margherita, Dorsoduro 2617

☎ 041 528 9420; church 041 296 0630

🕐 Apr–end Oct Mon–Sat 9–6, Sun 9–4; Nov–end Mar daily 9–4, (last admission 1 hour before closing)

🍴 Campo Santa Margherita

🚤 Ca' Rezzonico 1

♿ Poor: stairs to main rooms

💰 Moderate

❓ Visit the adjacent Chiesa dei Carmini 🕐 Mon–Sat 2.30–5.30 💰 Free

HIGHLIGHTS

● Façade
● Stucco staircase
● Ceiling paintings
● Albergo and Archivio
● *Judith and Holofernes*, Piazzetta
● *St. Nicholas of Bari*, Lorenzo Lotto
● *Nativity*, Cima da Conegliano

Giovanni Battista Tiepolo's paintings are not to all tastes, but those in the intimate Scuola Grande dei Carmini, all pastel shades and fleshy figures, are a pleasant change from the more obvious drama of Titian or Tintoretto.

Carmelites The Carmelite Order's Venetian chapter was originally installed in Santa Maria del Carmelo (or Carmini), the Carmelite church just to the left of the *scuola* (see below). In 1667 the order commissioned Baldassare Longhena to design a new home in the present building (Longhena also designed Santa Maria della Salute and a number of palaces on the Grand Canal).

Exuberant ceilings The highlights are Giovanni Battista Tiepolo's nine ceiling paintings (1739–44) in the Salone. The paintings' central panel depicts the vision of St. Simon Stock, elected the Carmelites' prior-general in 1247, in which the Virgin appears to the saint with a 'scapular'. This garment of two linked pieces of cloth became central to Carmelite belief as wearers were promised relief from the pains of purgatory on the 'first Sunday after death'. Two adjacent rooms, the Albergo and Archivio, have heavy wooden ceilings and several paintings, the best of which is Piazzetta's *Judith and Holofernes* (1743). Be sure to visit the Chiesa dei Carmini to see Lorenzo Lotto's *St. Nicholas of Bari* (1529), located by the side door (second chapel), and Cima da Conegliano's fine *Nativity* (1509) above the second altar on the opposite (south) wall.

More to See

CAMPO SANTA MARGHERITA

This may well become your preferred Venetian square, thanks mainly to its friendly and informal air, its collection of pleasant little bars and cafés, and its easy-going streetlife, which reminds you that Venice is still—just—a living city. Venetians meet here to chat, shop and sip coffee while their children play raucously on the square's ancient flag-stones. Causin (▷ 96), noted for its ice cream, is the longest established of the cafés, but Il Caffè and Il Doge are both equally fine places to sit and watch the world go by. San Pantalone (▷ 75), the Scuola Grande dei Carmini (▷ 90), San Sebastiano (▷ 88), the Scuola Grande di San Rocco (▷ 72–73) and Frari (▷ 70–71), the Accademia (▷ 86–87) and the Ca' Rezzonico (▷ 84) are all close by.
➕ E6 ✉ Dorsoduro 🍴 Cafés 🚤 Ca' Rezzonico 1

DOGANA DI MARE

The point where the Giudecca canal merges with the Grand Canal is known as the Punta della Dogana and is occupied by the Dogana di Mare. This replaced the original customs house near San Biagio in the 15th century and was reconstructed from 1677 to 1682 by Giuseppe Benoni. Warehouses stretch along the point, fronted by a portico below a small white tower. From this vantage point, every ship approaching the city could be observed. It's perhaps the finest panorama in Venice, with a view sweeping across the Bacino di San Marco and past San Giorgio Maggiore to the Piazza, while to the left the Grand Canal and its *palazzi* stretch.
➕ H7 ✉ Dogana di Mare, Dorsoduro 🚤 Salute 1

PALAZZO DARIO

The Palazzo Dario possesses perhaps the most charming façade of any Venetian palace, its appeal heightened by the building's rather alarming lean. Built in the 1480s, it was probably designed by Pietro Lombardo, whose use of inlaid marbles is repeated in his masterpiece, Santa Maria dei Miracoli (▷ 52). It has long been believed that

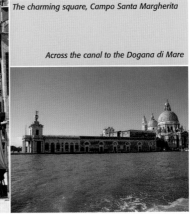

The charming square, Campo Santa Margherita

Across the canal to the Dogana di Mare

the Palazzo Dario is cursed. It is best viewed from the Grand Canal or the Santa Maria del Giglio landing stage opposite.

➕ G7 ✉ Calle Barbaro, Dorsoduro 352 🕐 Not open to the public 🚤 Giglio 1

PONTE DELL'ACCADEMIA

All the bridges across the Grand Canal (▷ 68–69) have mesmerizing views, but none perhaps as pretty as those from the Ponte dell'Accademia. Below you boats and gondolas flit about, while the Grand Canal curves gently to the east and west, with views of distant palaces and the church of Santa Maria della Salute (▷ 89).

➕ F7 ✉ Canal Grande 🚤 Accademia N, 1, 2, 4 ♿ Poor

SAN NICOLÒ DEI MENDICOLI

Charming San Nicolò was built in the 12th century and since 1966 has been restored by the Venice in Peril Fund. The interior is beautifully decorated with marbles, statues, paintings and fine gilded woodwork.

➕ C6 ✉ Campo San Nicolò dei Mendicoli, Dorsoduro 1907 ☎ 041 275 0382 🕐 Mon–Sat 10–12, 4–6 🚤 San Basilio N, 2, 61, 62 ♿ Good 🎫 Free

SQUERO DI SAN TROVASO

Venice had more than 10,000 gondolas in the 16th century; today there are only a few hundred, built in a handful of specialist boatyards, called *squeri.* One of the most famous, and easiest to see, is the Squero di San Trovaso, on the waterfront of the Rio San Trovaso, just behind the Zattere. Construction sheds and workshops are set back from the *rio,* and there's generally always activity of some sort, as gondolas are overhauled and repaired. Modern water conditions take a tremendous toll on the boats, which suffer particularly from the backwash of motorboats, and they need to be cleaned and overhauled as often as once a month. To get a real insight into the expertise of the gondolier, take a *traghetto* across the Grand Canal and watch the oarsmen.

➕ E7 ✉ Rio San Trovaso, Dorsoduro 🚤 Zattere N, 2, 51, 52, 61, 62

The view from the Ponte dell'Accademia toward Santa Maria della Salute

Peaceful setting for San Nicolò dei Mendicoli

Around Dorsoduro

Explore the hidden corners and alleys of the city, with some of the most interesting churches and museums, plus some sweeping vistas.

DISTANCE: 2km (1.2 miles) **ALLOW:** 3 hours with sights

START

CA' REZZONICO LANDING STAGE
⊞ E6 🚢 Ca' Rezzonico

END

PONTE DELL' ACCADEMIA
⊞ F7 🚢 Accademia

DORSODURO

WALK

❶ Alight at Ca' Rezzonico and walk down Calle Traghetto to Campo San Barnaba. Turn left under the *soto-portego* and follow this main route through Dorsoduro.

❷ Continue along Calle della Toletta to the Rio San Travaso. Cross Ponte delle Maragegie and turn right down the *fondamenta*, where you will see San Trovaso church.

❸ Across the water is the Squero di San Trovaso (▷ 92). At the end is the Fondamenta Zattere. Turn left and walk beside the Canale della Guidecca.

❹ You will come to the church of the Gesuiti (▷ 56). Continue along the Zattere, cross a bridge and continue to pass the church of Spirito Santo, founded in 1483.

❽ Turn right and follow the street to emerge in Campo San Vio. Bear left and cross the bridge into the Piscina del Forner then Calle Nuova Sant'Agnese; walk along this, then turn right to the Ponte dell' Accademia (▷ 92).

❼ Cross the bridge to reach Santa Maria della Salute (▷ 89). Retrace yours steps to the T-junction and cross the bridge. Follow the street to Campiello Barbaro. Walk round to the Fondamenta Venier to the Guggenheim gallery (▷ 85).

❻ Walk beside the Rio de la Fornace. At the end of this street, turn right and walk through a small *campo*, with the church of San Gregorio. Continue under the *sotogportego* (to the left).

❺ Continue to the next bridge, cross it and turn left.

93

Shopping

ANTICHITÀ

Beautiful antique beads and other jewellery, and a fine selection of small antiques, fabrics and lace. Choose your beads and have them made up on the spot, or bring beads for re-stringing.

E7 ✉ Calle Toletta, Dorsoduro 1195 ☎ 041 522 3159 🚤 Accademia N, 1, 2

BAC ART STUDIO

www.bacart.com

For some stunning photos of Venice to take home and prove to people that it really does look dreamlike, Bac Art Studio has an impressive range. There are also framed prints of original art, as well as stationery and calendars.

F7 ✉ San Vio, Dorsoduro 862 ☎ 041 522 8171 🚤 Accademia N, 1, 2

LE FORCOLE DI SAVERIO PASTOR

www.forcole.com

This gondola workshop also has a shop attached where you can buy either genuine gondola parts, wooden bookmarks, or scale models of forcole, which are the gondola's oar posts or rowlocks. They make really beautiful and very Venetian souvenirs to take home.

G7 ✉ Fondamenta Soranzo dette Fornace, Dorsoduro 341 ☎ 041 522 5699 🚤 Salute 1

GOBBETTI

It's easy to miss Gobbetti's entrance, just past the Ponte dei Pugni. This is the home of the best chocolate mousse cake in town, and a number of other superb sweet creations. There are miniature examples of all the big cakes, so you can sample the full range—try the fruit mousses or the cream tarts, delicately infused with green tea or lime.

E6 ✉ Rio Terrà Canal, Dorsoduro 3108B ☎ 041 528 9014 🚤 Ca' Rezzonico 1

LIBRERIA TOLETTA E TOLETTA STUDIO

The Libreria is an excellent bookshop with a huge range of coffee-table books on Venice, guidebooks, Italian classics, art and cookery books—and they're all offered with a 20 to 40 per cent discount. Across the calle, the Studio has more art books, posters, T-shirts and small gifts suitable for souvenirs.

E7 ✉ Calle Toletta,

SOUVENIRS

If you are hoping to take home some glass from Murano but have no time to visit try Susanna & Marina Sent (▷ this page). If there's no time to take a trip to Burano but lace is your thing there are some lovely examples at Annelie in the Calle Lunga Santa Barbara in Dorsoduro. Tablecloths, sheets and bed clothes at affordable prices.

Dorsoduro 1214 ☎ 041 523 2034 🚤 Ca' Rezzonico

MONDO NOVO

www.mondonovomaschere.it

The masks in this attractive shop, which is just south of Campo Santa Margherita, are definitely superior to the mediocre versions in lesser shops around the city. A wonderful place for children and adults alike.

E6 ✉ Rio Terrà Canal, Dorsoduro 3063 ☎ 041 528 7344 🚤 Ca' Rezzonico 1

PANTAGRUELICA

Pantagruelica is arguably the finest food shop in Venice, offering the best produce from all over Italy. The emphasis is on quality, with plenty of organic produce featured on the shelves. The enthusiastic owner is always happy to spend time talking about the food producers he patronizes.

E6 ✉ Campo San Barnaba, Dorsoduro 2844 ☎ 041 523 6766 🚤 Ca' Rezzonico 1

SUSANNA & MARINA SENT

For a more contemporary take on Murano glass, Marina and Susanna Sent have funky vases, plates and jewellery that won't break the bank. Lovely glass pebbles, too.

F7 ✉ Campo San Vio, Dorsoduro 669 ☎ 041 520 8136 11–6 🚤 Accademia N, 1, 2

Entertainment and Nightlife

CANTINA DEL VINO GIÀ SCHIAVI

An old-fashioned wine bar that really looks the part, set almost opposite San Trovaso and one of Venice's few remaining gondola workshops.

🔒 E7 ✉ Fondamenta Nani-Meravegie, Dorsoduro 992 ☎ 041 523 0034 🕐 Closed Sun pm 🚤 Accademia or Zattere N, 1, 2, 51, 52, 61, 62

CODROMA

Generations of Venetians —artist, workers, students—have come to Codroma for over a century to take a coffee, glass of wine or snack, settling down on wooden benches in comfortable, easygoing surroundings.

🔒 D6 ✉ Fondamenta Briati, near Calle dei Gaurdiani, Dorsoduro 2540 ☎ 041 524 6789 🕐 Mon–Sat 9–1 🚤 San Basilio N, 2, 61, 62

ORANGE

www.orangebar.it
Orange spritz is the signature drink here in this orange-theme bar, restaurant and champagne lounge. There's an upstairs terrace, to watch life on the Campo, but most of the achingly chic drinkers are too busy watching each other.

🔒 E6 ✉ Campo Santa Margherita 3054a ☎ 041 523 4740 🕐 Daily 8am–2am 🚤 Ca' Rezzonico 1

PICCOLO MONDO

Not the most hip, but one of Venice's only discos.

🔒 F7 ✉ Calle Contarini Corfù, Dorsoduro 1056/a ☎ 041 520 0371 🕐 Tue–Sun 11pm–4am 🚤 Accademia N, 1, 2

RIVIERA

www.ristoranteriviera.it
One of the best among the restaurants on the Zattere, if a little pricier than some. It is a delightful place to eat and then settle back with a drink outside on summer evenings.

🔒 D7 ✉ Fondamente Zattere Ponte Lungo, corner of Calle del Masena, Dorsoduro 1473 ☎ 041 522 7621 🕐 Closed Sun 🚤 Accademia or Zattere N, 1, 2, 51, 52, 61, 62

ROUND MIDNIGHT

This intimate club attracts all sorts for the mainstream music.

CARNEVALE

Venice's famous carnival takes its name from the Latin *carnem levare*, or *carne vale*—the 'farewell to meat'. It probably began in the city's 15th-century private clubs. Resurrected in 1979 (by a group of non-Venetians), it emulates the great pre-Lenten festivals of the 18th century, thousands of tourists dressing in masks and extravagant costumes to indulge in a series of enthusiastically supported events. Today, the carnival officially lasts just 10 days (up to the beginning of Lent).

🔒 E6 ✉ Calle dei Pugli, off Fondamenta dello Squero, Dorsoduro 3102 ☎ 041 523 2056 🕐 Mon, Wed–Sat 10pm–4am 🚤 Ca' Rezzonico 1

SANTA MARIA DELLA SALUTE

The venue for a variety of classical organ music. As well as performances by the lead organist of the Basilica, guest performers also appear as part of Sunday Mass at 11am every week.

🔒 G7 ✉ Campo della Salute, Dorsoduro 1 ☎ 041 522 5558 🕐 Phone for latest details 🚤 Salute 1

SUZIE CAFÉ

Popular with students in the day, this place transforms into a swinging bar at night. On Friday jazz, reggae or funk bands perform.

🔒 D7 ✉ Campo San Basegio, Dorsoduro 1527A–B ☎ 041 522 7502 🕐 Mon–Thu 7–7, Fri–Sat 8am–1am (if there's a concert in the Campo) 🚤 Zattere N, 1, 2, 51, 52, 61, 62

TEATRO DA L'AVOGARIA

www.teatroavogaria.it
This experimental theatre was founded in 1969 by director Giovanni Poli. It continues to stage works by little-known, 15th- to 19th-century playwrights.

🔒 D6 ✉ Corte Zappa, Dorsoduro 1617 ☎ 041 520 9270 🕐 Phone for details 🎟 Voluntary donation 🚤 San Basilio N, 2, 61, 62

Restaurants

PRICES

Prices are approximate, based on a 3-course meal for one person.

€€€	over €55
€€	€35–€55
€	under €35

ANTICA MONTIN (€€€)

This venerable restaurant has been famous for several decades and is popular with the rich and famous, although today it depends somewhat on its former reputation. The quality of food is now once again touching former heights; an evocative place to eat, either in the painting-lined dining room or on the shaded outside terrace to the rear.

➕ E7 ✉ Fondamenta di Borgo, Dorsoduro 1147 ☎ 041 522 7151 🕐 Closed Wed, Tue dinner 🚤 Zattere or Ca' Rezzonico N, 1, 2, 51, 52

LA BITTA (€€)

La Bitta has an attractive bottle-filled dining room and internal courtyard, opening along its length. Serves mainly meat-based dishes.

➕ E6 ✉ Calle Lunga San Barnaba, Dorsoduro 2753/a ☎ 041 523 0531 🕐 Closed Sun and lunch 🚤 Ca' Rezzonico 1

CAUSIN (€)

Opened in 1928, this is one of several excellent cafés on Venice's nicest square. Great ice cream and outdoor tables.

➕ E6 ✉ Campo Santa Margherita, Dorsoduro 2996 ☎ 041 523 6091 🕐 Daily 6am–9pm 🚤 Ca' Rezzonico 1

DONA ONESTA (€€€)

www.donaonesta.com

The 'Honest Woman' lives up to its name with fine food at budget prices. It is becoming increasingly well known, however, so try to reserve a table in its single small dining room. Overlooks a little canal midway between San Pantalon and San Tomà.

➕ E5 ✉ Calle della Donna Onesta, Dorsoduro 3922 ☎ 041 710 586 🕐 Daily 🚤 San Tomà N, 1, 2

HARRY'S DOLCI (€€€)

www.cipriani.com

Fancy a trip over to the island of Guidecca? What

COFFEE

At breakfast you will be served a milky cappuccino, which Italians rarely drink after midday. During the rest of the day the locals' coffee of choice is the short, black espresso or *un caffè*. A longer espresso is a *lungo* or a *doppia* (double). American-style coffee (not as strong as the Italian brews) is *un caffè Americano*. Other varieties include iced coffee (*caffè freddo*), *caffè corretto* (with a dash of grappa or brandy), *caffè latte* (a milky coffee) and *caffè macchiato* (an espresso 'stained' with a drop of milk).

began as a glorified cake- and coffee-shop offshoot of Harry's Bar has turned into a canalside restaurant with great views every bit as good (and almost as expensive) as its parent. The refined food is Venetian, while the atmosphere is chic without being at all intimidating. You can still just get a coffee or afternoon tea.

➕ D8 ✉ Fondamenta San Biagio, Giudecca 773 ☎ 041 522 4844 🕐 Apr–end Oct daily 10.30–3pm, 7.30–10.30pm, Nov–end Mar closed Tue 🚤 Palanca N, 2, 41, 42

NICO (€)

Organize a walk or stroll the Dorsoduro district so that you pass this small waterfront bar renowned for its ice cream, in particular a praline concoction known as *gianduiotto*.

➕ E8 ✉ Zattere ai Gesuati, Dorsoduro 922 ☎ 041 522 5293 🕐 Closed Thu 🚤 Zattere N, 2, 51, 52, 61, 62

TAVERNA SAN TROVASO (€)

www.tavernasantrovaso.it

Not the best cuisine in the city, yet it has reliable cooking at reasonable prices. Popular with Venetians, and its position west of the Accademia attracts passing trade. Make a reservation to be sure of a place (especially for Sunday lunch).

➕ E7 ✉ Fondamenta Priuli, Dorsoduro 1016 ☎ 041 520 3703 🕐 Closed Mon 🚤 Accademia N, 1, 2

If you feel the heat or have had enough of the crowds in Venice, there is the perfect trip close by. The islands have their individual appeal and for those who want the beach the Lido is just a boat ride away.

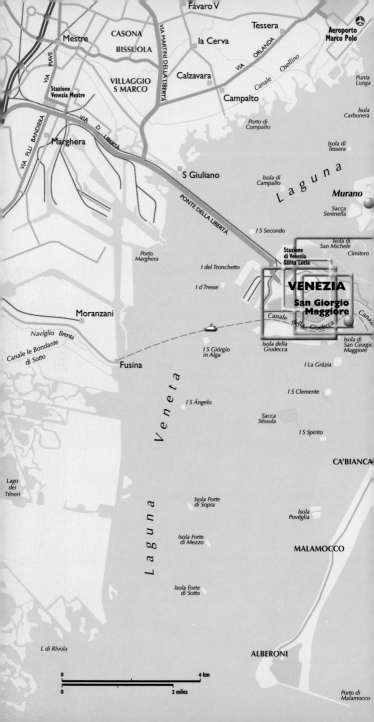

la Cura

Palude
della Rossa

Palude della Centrega

Palude
del Monte

Torcello

Palude
del Tralo

Isola Buèl
del Lovo

Mazzorbo

Burano

Isola Madonna
del Monte

V e n e t a

Ca'
Bubacco

la Ricettoría

Isola S Giácomo
in Palude

Ca' la
Vela

Ca' Tiépolo

**Sant'
Erasmo**

Litorale di S Erasmo

Canale di Treporti

Punta
Sabbioni

Ca'
Cavara

le Vignole

Ca' Sávio

Vignole

Punta Sabbioni

Idroscalo
S Andrea

Isola di
San Pietro

la
Certosa

Litorale del Cavallino

S NICOLÒ

Isola di
Sant'Elena

S Marco

Isola S
Sérvolo

Porto
di Lido

sola S Lázzaro
degli Armeni

Lido

Isola
Lazzaretto
Vécchio

Lido

Litorale del Lido

Ízmir
Kérkyra
Igoumenitsa
Pátra

LA ROTONDA

FARTHER AFIELD ⭐ TOP 25

Glassmaking on Murano (left) and the results (middle); Santa Maria e Donato (right)

Murano

The lagoon island of Murano is a miniature Venice, and has been the historic heart of Venetian glass production for over 800 years, reaching its peak between the 15th and 16th centuries.

Seeing Murano It's a 10-minute trip across the lagoon to Murano, a self-contained community with its own Grand Canal, fine churches, *palazzi* and glassblowing industry. There are numerous privately run excursions from the city, but for good value and flexibility make the trip independently via the *vaporetti*. Allow two to three hours for a thorough visit. It's quite feasible, given an early start, to combine a visit to Murano with a trip to the northern islands of Burano and Torcello; study the *vaporetto* timetable with care as onward connections run half-hourly only.

Highlights The glass factories are well worth a visit but bear in mind the majority are closed on Saturday and Sunday. A glassmaking hub since 1291, Murano has three major sights over and above its ubiquitous glass workshops and showrooms. The first is the church of San Pietro Martire noted for Giovanni Bellini's altarpiece. Also well worth seeing is the Museo del Vetro, Italy's only glass museum, with displays of objects dating from Roman times. Just beyond lies the church of Santa Maria e Donato, distinguished by a striking arched and colonnaded apse. Inside, the 12th-century apse mosaic of the Madonna is outstanding, as are the swirling tinted patterns of the lovely mosaic floor (1141).

THE BASICS

🔲 b2
✉ Isola di Murano
🚢 5, 13, LN, 41, 42, DM every 60–90 mins from Fondamente Nuove

Museo del Vetro
🔲 b2 ✉ Fondamenta Giustinian 8 ☎ 041 739 586 🕐 Apr–end Oct Thu–Tue 10–6; Nov–end Mar Thu–Tue 10–5
👆 Moderate 🚢 Museo

Santa Maria e Donato
🔲 c2 ✉ Campo San Donato 🕐 Mon–Sat 9–12, 3.30–7, Sun 3.30–7
👆 Free 🚢 Museo

HIGHLIGHTS
- Glass factories
- Museo del Vetro
- Santa Maria e Donato

San Giorgio Maggiore

The view from the Campanile is spell-binding, but if asked their best viewpoint many Venetians would probably nominate the bell tower of San Giorgio Maggiore, a magnificent Palladian church near the Giudecca.

Classical The church's dazzling marble façade provides one of the great panoramic set pieces of the Venetian skyline. Founded in 790, the first church on the site was destroyed by an earth-quake in 1223, together with an adjoining Benedictine monastery built in 982. While the monastery was rebuilt in 1443, the church had to wait until 1559 and the arrival of the great Vicenzan architect, Andrea Palladio. His design for the new church adopted many of the architectural idioms of the ancient world (notably the majestic

The striking marble exterior of the church of San Giorgio Maggiore (left); intricate carving between the columns (top middle); an imposing skyline (below middle); the magnificent painting The Stoning of St. Stephen by Jacopo and Domenico Tintertto inside the church (right)

four-column portico) to produce one of Italy's most beautiful neoclassical buildings.

Interior The ancient world also influenced the sparse interior, where light is introduced by high windows, a device borrowed from the bathhouses of 3rd-century Rome. The major works of art are Jacopo Bassano's famous *Adoration of the Shepherds* (1582), located above the second altar on the right, and a pair of outstanding paintings by Tintoretto—*The Fall of Manna* (1594) and *The Last Supper* (1594)—located on the walls of the chancel. Also worth a look is the church's choir (1594–98), tucked away behind the high altar and the stalls are impressive. All else in the church pales, however, alongside the breathtaking view from the campanile, reached by an elevator at the end of the north aisle.

THE BASICS

✚ K8
✉ Campo San Giorgio, Isola di San Giorgio Maggiore
☎ 041 522 7827
🕐 Daily 9.30–12.30, 2.30–4.30 (6.30 May–end Sep). Times can vary (particularly in winter)
🍴 Giudecca
🚤 San Giorgio N, 2
♿ Poor
💷 Campanile moderate

Torcello

The sights of Torcello range from beautiful churches to tranquil scenery

THE BASICS

➕ Off map to northeast

🚢 LN from Fondamente Nuove to Burano then 'T' boat to Torcello, every 60–90 min; takes 45 min. Get the earliest boat to avoid a crowd

Museo dell'Estuario

☎ 041 270 2464

🕐 Mar–end Oct Tue–Sun 10.30–5.30; Nov–end Feb 10–5 👷 Inexpensive

Basilica di Santa Maria Assunta

☎ 041 296 0630

🕐 Mar–end Oct daily 10.30–6; Nov–end Mar 10–5 👷 Church and bell tower inexpensive. Moderate for combined ticket

HIGHLIGHTS

● Basilica di Santa Maria Assunta
● Santa Fosca church
● View from the campanile

The evocative rural backwater of Torcello, dreaming in the past, is Venice's most ancient settlement and the site of a superb basilica, the oldest building in the lagoon.

Seeing Torcello From the landing stage a path runs beside Torcello's canal, crossed by the simple stone span of the Ponte del Diavolo (Devil's Bridge), to the main piazza. Around here everything there is to see is grouped. You will also find the so-called Trono di Attila, a primitive stone chair once used by the bishop.

Island churches One of the most magical places in Venice, Torcello was probably the city's birthplace and the first area of the lagoon settled in the 5th century. Malaria and the silting up of its canals snuffed out its prosperity in the 12th century, and today it is home to little more than a single hamlet and a beautiful patchwork of green fields and leafy canals dominated by the cathedral of Santa Maria Assunta, Venice's oldest building (founded 639) and one of its loveliest sights as well as the finest Veneto-Byzantine church in Italy. The lofty interior, bare and cool, has some superb moasics from the 9th to 12th centuries, on the vaults and walls. Climb the bell-tower for wonderful lagoon views across the mudflats and marsh. Also worth seeing close by are the 11th-century Byzantine church of Santa Fosca and the small Museo dell'Estuario, which houses a low-key display of archaelogical finds from Torcello and the lagoon. The perfect antedote to the crowds and heat of Venice.

More to See

BURANO

In the Museo del Merletto you can see breathtaking intricate examples of traditional lace. The island's fame in part rests on its many brightly painted houses, whose wonderful bold statements make its streets and canals as picturesque as Venice itself. Fishing boats moor at the island's fringes and nets are laid out to dry by the road, and despite the faint air of commercialism and the many visitors, it feels like a genuine fishing community.

 a4–c5 Isola di Burano LN (Laguna Nord) from Fondamente Nuove, every 60–90 min

Museo del Merletto b5 Piazza Galuppi 187 ☎ 041 730 034 Wed–Mon 10–5 (Nov–end Mar 10–4) Moderate

THE LIDO

The island of the Lido is essentially a long, narrow, sandbank, once a sparsely inhabited island of dunes and pinewoods. Today it combines its role as a residential suburb with that of a seaside resort and overspill hotel area for Venice. A 10-minute boat trip from the city will bring you to a different world, where cars, buses and supermarkets are the backdrop to lazy beach days. If you like more active pursuits, there are tennis courts, a golf course, as well as walking and cycling.

 Off map to southeast Gran Viale Santa Maria Elisabetta 6a, Lido di Venezia ☎ 041 526 5721 Jun–end Sep daily 9–12.30, 3.30–6 Lido

SANT'ERASMO

Bigger than Venice itself, Sant'Erasmo is one of the lagoon's best-kept secrets. It lies northeast of the city, a long, flat, sparsely inhabited island where sandy paths crisscross well-kept fields and tiny vineyards. Sant'Erasmo produces huge quantities of vegetables for the city markets. The island is traversed by a single road, where rickety old unlicensed cars trundle up and down. The island does have a tiny store at the main settlement, built around the church, and a couple of *trattorie*.

 Off map to northeast Isola di Sant' Erasmo Capannone, Chiesa, Punta Vela 13

Picturesque and brightly painted houses in Burano

Down at the beach—take a welcome break at the Lido

It's not easy to find accommodation at reasonable prices in one of the world's top tourist destinations, so expect to pay a price. It's imperative to book well in advance and try checking the internet for bargains.

Where to Stay

Introduction

Compared with its population, Venice has more tourist accommodation than any other Italian city. This ranges from the five-star luxury of some of the world's greatest hotels to the rather bland modern chain hotels and simple, low-key *pensioni*. Despite this, the city remains a seller's market, popular at all times of year, and this is reflected in the high prices of all its accommodation.

What to Expect
Italy's hotels, including those in Venice, are classified by the state system into five categories, from one star (basic) to five stars (luxury). The prices of individual rooms should be displayed in the entrance hall and in the room itself. Prices for different rooms often vary within a hotel, so if a room is too expensive be sure to ask if another is available for less (you may well be shown the most expensive room first). Watch out for supplements for breakfast, which may be charged even if you do not take it, and in peak periods remember that hotels may insist that you take half- or full board.

Where to Stay
San Marco, at the heart of the action, has lots of places to stay but is also constantly crowded and noisy by day. To the west Cannaregio is a good bet and cheaper, but much accommodation is around the rail station. East of San Marco Castello has much to offer; it's more remote, quieter and you pay far less. Across the Grand Canal, Santa Croce and San Polo have plenty of choice, particulary around the Rialto. Hotels here tend to be family-run, smallish places with Venetian-style traditional rooms. Dorsoduro is another good choice, with quiet canals and a more residential atmosphere.

FEELING THE HEAT

Venice is very hot in the summer, so a courtyard or garden is a bonus, as are rooms away from the street. Bear in mind that noise bounces off water and narrow streets, especially if they are major thoroughfares.

There is plenty of scope for a more individual stay in the city of Venice

PRICES

Expect to pay between €90 and €175 per night for a budget hotel.

AI DO MORI

www.hotelaidomori.it
A friendly, 11-room hotel with just eight bathrooms in a busy spot close to San Marco. Room prices vary: the best on the upper floors are small but have views over the Basilca di San Marco.
➕ J6 ✉ Calle Larga San Marco, San Marco 658 ☎ 041 520 4817 or 041 528 9293; fax 041 520 5328 🚢 Vallaresso N, 1, 2 or all services to San Zaccaria

ALEX

www.hotelalexinvenice.com
This one-star hotel's excellent location near Santa Maria Gloriosa dei Frari and the Scuola Grande di San Rocco makes up for the slightly tired and rather dated 11 rooms.
➕ F5 ✉ Rio Terrà Frari, San Polo 2606 ☎ 041 523 1341; fax 041 523 1341 🚢 San Tomà N, 1, 2

ANTICO CAPON

www.anticocapon.com
Seven simple rooms (six with bathroom) on one of Venice's most informal squares. Excellent location for sightseeing.
➕ E6 ✉ Campo Santa Margherita, Dorsoduro 3004/b ☎ 041 528 5292; fax 041 528 5292 🚢 San Tomà or Ca' Rezzonico N, 1, 2

CA' FOSCARI

www.locandacafoscari.com
This relaxed and well-appointed one-star hotel has 10 rooms (five with private bathroom) and is hidden away in an alley.
➕ E6 ✉ Calle della Frescada, Dorsoduro 3888/b ☎ 041 710 401; fax 041 710 817 🚢 San Tomà or Ca' Rezzonico N, 1, 2

CANADA

www.canadavenice.com
This immaculate 25-room hotel has several singles. The best room (a double) has its own roof terrace. Reserve in advance.
➕ J5 ✉ Campo San Lio, Castello 5659 ☎ 041 522 9912; fax 041 523 5852 🚢 Rialto N, 1, 2, 4

DA BRUNO

www.hoteldabruno.com
An excellent location close to the Rialto outweighs the small size

NOISE

Although Venice is remarkably quiet, it still has its fair share of nocturnal traffic-- even without cars. Church bells clang through the night and pedestrian chatter in the main alleys and streets is amplified in the close quarters. Traffic on the main canals can also be surprisingly noisy, and refuse boats, *vaporetti* and food suppliers start up very early. This can put a different complexion on that desirable room overlooking the Grand Canal.

of the hotel's 32 rooms.
➕ J5 ✉ Salizzada San Lio, Castello 5726/a ☎ 041 523 0452; fax 041 522 1157 🚢 Rialto N, 1, 2, 4

DONI

www.albergodoni.it
Intimate one-star hotel in an attractive spot between the Basilica and San Zaccaria, Some of the 13 clean, simple rooms (four with private bathroom) overlook the Riva del Vin or the small garden.
➕ K6 ✉ Calle del Vin, off Salizzada San Provolo, Castello 4656 ☎ 041 522 4267; fax 041 522 4267 🚢 All services to San Zaccaria

FIORITA

www.locandafiorita.com
Very pretty, popular hotel in a quaint square (used for breakfast in summer) just north of Santo Stefano. The 10 rooms (all with private bath) have beamed ceilings.
➕ F6 ✉ Campiello Novo, San Marco 3457/a ☎ 041 523 4754; fax 041 522 8043 🚢 Accademia or Sant'Angelo N, 1, 2, 4

MONTIN

www.locandamontin.com
Much of this popular hotel's fame derives from the well-known restaurant of the same name downstairs. The 10 rooms (some with private bathroom) are pleasant.
➕ E7 ✉ Fondamenta di Borgo, Dorsoduro 1147 ☎ 041 522 7151; fax 041 520 0255 🚢 Ca' Rezzonico or Accademia N, 1, 2, 4

Mid-Range Hotels

PRICES

Expect to pay between €175 and €300 per night for a mid-range hotel.

ACCADEMIA-VILLA MARAVEGE

www.pensioneaccademia.it
A 17th-century *palazzo*, west of the Accademia that once housed the Russian Embassy. Its 25 rooms are grand and furnished with antiques, although some are small. The garden has a Grand Canal view.
⊞ E7 ✉ Fondamenta Bollani, Dorsoduro 1058 ☎ 041 521 0188; fax 041 523 9152 🚉 Accademia N, 1, 2

AGLI ALBORETTI

www.aglialboretti.com
This 23-room hotel was added to the fine restaurant downstairs. Located on a tree-lined street and convenient to the Accademia and Zattere. Rooms are modern and stylish, if a little small, and there is a pleasant garden. Extremely popular.
⊞ F7 ✉ Rio Terrà Sant'Agnese-Antonio Foscarini, Dorsoduro 884 ☎ 041 523 0058; fax 041 521 0158 🚉 Accademia or Zattere N, 1, 2

AL PIAVE

www.hotelalpiave.com
This 27-room hotel is located near Campo Santa Maria Formosa and offers good value for Venice. A very sleek, art deco inspired lobby welcomes guests.
⊞ J5 ✉ Ruga Giuffa, San Marco 4838–50 ☎ 041 528 5174; fax 041 523 8512 🚉 San Marco, Rialto N, 1, 82

AMERICAN

www.hotelamerican.com
A 29-room hotel two minutes' walk from the Accademia, on a small canal away from the crowds. Rooms vary in price and quality but most have a lot of wood and period touches. Lovely terrace and vine-shaded breakfast area.
⊞ F7 ✉ Fondamenta Bragadin, Rio di San Vio, Dorsoduro 628 ☎ 041 520 4733; fax 041 520 4048 🚉 Accademia N, 1, 2

CAMPIELLO

www.hcampiello.it
This three-star hotel is

TIGHT SQUEEZE

Venice has been accommodating visitors for hundreds of years, although over the last couple of decades the sheer number of tourists to the city has strained its 200 or so hotels to capacity, and brought about a slide in standards among the more cynical hoteliers (who know they are guaranteed customers however grim their properties). Prices are also higher than in most of Italy and reservations are now a virtual necessity all year around. Noise, location and actually finding a room are other important considerations.

near the most popular San Marco sights. The bright and cheery hall, breakfast room and bar have marble floors and elegant furnishings. The 17 bedrooms are comfortable and functional.
⊞ K6 ✉ Campiello del Vin, Castello 4647 ☎ 041 520 5764 🚉 San Zaccaria N, 1, 2, 41, 42, 51, 52, LN

CASANOVA

www.hotelcasanova.it
This comfortable hotel has 50 rooms and is close to Piazza San Marco. Mostly modern bedrooms but the public spaces have fine old furniture and vast antique mirrors.
⊞ H6 ✉ Frezzeria, San Marco 1284 ☎ 041 520 6855; fax 041 520 6413 🚉 Vallaresso N, 1, 2

FALIER

www.hotelfalier.com
A small, well-presented two-star hotel in a part of town that is less busy, but convenient for Santa Maria Gloriosa dei Frari and the Scuola Grande di San Rocco. Some of the 19 rooms (all with private bathrooms and nonsmoking) are small, but all are elegant and tidy.
⊞ E5 ✉ Salizzada San Pantalon, Santa Croce 130 ☎ 041 710882; fax 041 520 6554 🚉 San Tomà N, 1, 2 or services to Ferrovi

FLORA

www.hotelflora.it
This 44-room hotel has a well-deserved reputation,

thanks to its pleasant garden. Some rooms are rather small. Just off the south side of Calle Larga (Viale) XXII Marzo west of Piazza San Marco.
✚ G7 ✉ Calle Bergamaschi, San Marco 2283a ☎ 041 520 5844; fax 041 522 8217 🚤 Giglio 1

KETTE
www.hotelkette.com
Quiet location just southeast of La Fenice opera house. Some of the 63 four-star rooms are small for the price, but rates can be reasonable off-season.
✚ G6 ✉ Piscina San Moisè, San Marco 2053 ☎ 041 520 7766; fax 041 522 8964 🚤 Vallaresso or Giglio N, 1, 2

LA CALCINA
www.lacalcina.com
The waterfront location of this 29-room hotel may not be to all tastes, but you are in an interesting area of the city well away from the bustle.
✚ F8 ✉ Fondamenta Zattere ai Gesuati and Fondamenta Vernier, Dorsoduro 780 ☎ 041 520 6466; fax 041 522 7045 🚤 Zattere 2, 51, 52, 61, 62

LA FENICE ET DES ARTISTES
www.fenicehotels.com
Pleasant four-star hotel with 69 rooms divided into two buildings: rooms are modern and bland in one, elegant in the other.
✚ G6 ✉ Campiello Fenice, San Marco 1936 ☎ 041 523 2333; fax 041 520 3721 🚤 Giglio 1

LOCANDA LA CORTE
www.locandalacorte.it
This delightful hotel was home to a Venetian noble family in the 16th century, and its 16 rooms maintain a historic and luxurious look but with modern amenities. The inner courtyard, where breakfast is taken, is a special treat.
✚ J5 ✉ Calle Bressana, Castello 6317 ☎ 041 241 1300; fax 041 241 5982 🚤 Fondamente Nuove 52

PENSIONE SEGUSO
www.pensioneseguso.it
A better choice than the nearby Calcina (▷ this page), since most of its 36 traditionally furnished rooms have canal views.
✚ F8 ✉ Fondamenta Zattere ai Gesuati, Dorsoduro 779 ☎ 041 528 6858;

RESERVATIONS
It is now almost essential to reserve a room in Venice for July and August, and wise to do so during the rest of the peak season, which officially runs from 15 March to 15 November and from 21 December to 6 January, and now in effect includes the period of *Carnevale* in February. Many hotels do not recognize a low season, however, and lower category hotels where you might have been able to negotiate lower off-season rates often close in winter. Check out the internet for best deals.

fax 041 522 2340 🚤 Zattere N, 2, 51, 52

ROYAL SAN MARCO
www.sanmarcohotels.com
This 42-room three-star hotel is on one of Venice's main shopping streets within easy reach of Piazza San Marco. Rooms vary in terms of furnishings and views; most are smallish, but comfortable.
✚ H6 ✉ Calle dei Fabbri, San Marco 848 ☎ 041 528 7665; fax 041 522 6628 🚤 Rialto or Vallaresso N, 1, 2, 4

SAN CASSIANO-CA' FAVRETTO
www.sancassiano.it
A lovely three-star hotel full of charm, in a converted 14th-century *palazzo* on the Grand Canal almost opposite the Ca' d'Oro. Half the 36 rooms face the Grand Canal, the rest look on to a side canal.
✚ G4 ✉ Calle della Rosa, Santa Croce 2232 ☎ 041 524 1768; fax 041 721033 🚤 San Stae N, 1

SANTA MARINA
www.hotelsantamarina.it
Comfortable four-star hotel that lies off the tourist trail, but is still convenient for shopping and major sights. The 40 bright rooms are in Venetian period style.
✚ H11 ✉ Campo di Santa Marina, Castello 6068 ☎ 041 523 9202; fax 041 520 0907 🚤 Rialto N, 1, 2, 4

WHERE TO STAY MID-RANGE HOTELS

Luxury Hotels

PRICES

Expect to pay between €300 and €600 per night for a luxury hotel

BAUER

www.bauervenezia.it
Not as famous as other hotels in its class, but almost as stylish and elegant. Restoration has transformed this Grand Canal institution. The Bauer 'hotel' occupies a modern wing and the sumptious 'Palazzo' boutique hotel is housed in an 18th-century palace.
✚ H6 ✉ Campo San Moisé, San Marco 1459 ☎ 041 520 7022; fax 041 520 7557 ⛴ Vallaresso 1, 2

DANIELI

www.luxurycollection.com
A hotel since 1822, the Danieli is the choice of visiting royalty and VIPs. It ranks as the finest of Venice's luxury hotels—but stay in the old wing of the Gothic palazzo rather than the newer annexe. 233 rooms and suites.
✚ J6 ✉ Riva degli Schiavoni-Calle delle Rasse, Castello 4196 ☎ 041 522 6480; fax 041 520 0208 ⛴ San Zaccaria 1, 2

EUROPA E REGINA

www.westin.com
Venice's 'Big Three'—the Gritti, Cipriani and Danieli—tend to overshadow this Westin-owned hotel, but its prices are some of the most reasonable of the city's luxury hotels. Most of the 192 rooms are spacious and many enjoy glorious views
✚ H7 ✉ Off Calle Larga (Viale) XXII Marzo, San Marco 2159 ☎ 041 240 0001; fax 041 523 1533 ⛴ Vallaresso or Giglio N, 1, 2

GIORGIONE

www.hotelgiorgione.com
A 76-room hotel with modern facilities; one of the best in the category. Rooms are in period style, with elegant fabrics and attention to fine detail.
✚ H4 ✉ Campo Santi Apostoli, Cannaregio 4587 ☎ 041 522 5810; fax 041 523 9092 ⛴ Ca' d'Oro 1

GRITTI PALACE

www.starwoodhotels.com
Not the most expensive hotel in Venice, but—along with the Danieli—the one traditionally

CIPRIANI

Venice's most expensive hotel is a relative newcomer, having opened in 1963, but has quickly become a byword for luxury. The location in gardens on the eastern end of the Giudecca is away from the tourist hustle, but can make you feel slightly isolated from the city. Virtually all 104 rooms (50 suites) have superb views.
✉ Giudecca 10 ☎ 041 520 7744; fax 041 520 3930; www.hotelcipriani.it
⛴ Zitelle N, 41, 42, 82
❓ Private launch service

considered to have the most class and élan. Greta Garbo and Winston Churchill are among its past guests. Housed in a 15th-century palazzo close to the Grand Canal, its 91 rooms and reception areas are all impeccably grand, as is the service. A private launch and private beach, adding a personal touch, are both available.
✚ G7 ✉ Campo Santa Maria del Giglio ☎ 041 794611; fax 041 520 0942 ⛴ Giglio 1

LUNA HOTEL BAGLIONI

www.baglionihotels.com
The five-star luxury Luna Hotel is perhaps not as well known as Venice's other big names but it matches them for quality and is said to be the oldest in the city. A hotel has been on this site since the 12th century, when the Knights Templars stayed here. Today its 104 rooms and suites spread across five floors and have 18th-century style furniture, marble bathrooms, Murano glass chandeliers and other sumptuous touches.
✚ J6 ✉ San Marco 1243 ☎ 041 528 9840; fax 041 528 7160 ⛴ Vallaresso N, 1, 2

WHERE TO STAY LUXURY HOTELS

Need to Know

This section offers all you need to know about Venice, from how to pay your *traghetti* fare to where to go to send an e-mail, to opening hours and health precautions—all the ins and outs of a visit.

Planning Ahead

When to Go

Avoid July and August, the hottest and busiest months, and plan a visit for April (excluding the busy Easter period), May, June, September or October. Hotels are busy from Easter to October, in February during *Carnevale*, and over Christmas and New Year. Despite the weather, winter can still be a delightful time to see the city.

TIME
Italy is one hour ahead of GMT in winter, six hours ahead of New York and nine hours ahead of Los Angeles.

AVERAGE DAILY MAXIMUM TEMPERATURES

JAN	FEB	MAR	APR	MAY	JUN	JUL	AUG	SEP	OCT	NOV	DEC
43°F	46°F	54°F	59°F	66°F	73°F	79°F	79°F	70°F	61°F	54°F	45°F
6°C	8°C	12°C	15°C	20°C	23°C	26°C	25°C	21°C	16°C	12°C	7°C

Spring (March to May) has a mixture of sunshine and showers, the chill easterly wind, the *bora*, can lower temperatures. Fog occurs occasionally.

Summer (June to August) can be unpredictable; clear skies and searing heat one day followed by sultry cloud and thunderstorms the next.

Autumn (September to November) becomes wetter as the season progresses and fog can envelope the city. Again, the *bora* can create a noticeable wind chill.

Winter (December to February) is generally mild but flooding, *acqua alta*, can occur.

WHAT'S ON

February *Carnevale* (carnival): Pageants, masks and costumes.

March *Su e zo per i ponti*: A long road race in which competitors run 'up and down the bridges' of Venice (fourth Sunday in Lent).

April *Festa di San Marco*: A gondola race from Sant'Elena to the Punta della Dogana marks the feast day of Venice's patron saint. Men traditionally give women a red rose.

May *La Sensa*: Venice's mayor reenacts the Marriage to the Sea, in which the doge would cast a ring into the sea to symbolize the 'wedding' of the city to the sea (Sunday after Ascension Day). *Vogalonga*: Literally the 'long row', a 32km (20-mile) race from Piazza San Marco to Burano and back (one Sunday in May).

June *Biennale*: Venice's international art exhibition takes place every odd-numbered year (Jun–Sep).

July *Festa del Redentore*: Pontoons are laid across the Giudecca canal to the Redentore to celebrate Venice's deliverance from the plague of 1576. People picnic in boats and watch fireworks (third Sunday of the month).

September *Venice Film Festival*: Held on the Lido (late Aug/early Sep). *Regata Storica*: Historical costume pageant and procession of boats on the Canal Grande, followed by a race among gondoliers (first Sunday of the month).

November *Festa della Salute*: A pontoon is built across the Canal Grande, to the Salute, to celebrate the passing of a plague in 1630 (21 Nov).

Useful Websites

www.enit.it
The main Italian Tourist Board website carries a wealth of information on everything you need to know about the whole country, with Venice getting plenty of attention. The site is available in several languages.

www.emmeti.it
Another Italy-based site, in English and Italian, with a good range of information on Venice, and links to other sites. It's strong on local events and offers an online hotel booking service.

www.turismovenezia.it
This excellent site, in English and Italian, gives a wealth of information on every aspect of the city. You'll find details of accommodation, restaurants and shopping as well as the full lowdown on what to see and do. There's a frequently updated newsletter and good links to other sites.

www.comune.venezia.it
Although aimed as much at local residents as visitors, the Venetian city council's site provides good up-to-date information on cultural activities and historic sites in the city. Look here for the latest on erratically opening museums, city services and what's on when.

www.venezia.net
Italian site with English version. News, general travel information, shopping, a selection of bars, cafés and restaurants, excellent material on museums and main attractions, plus 3-D tours of sights.

www.veniceforvisitors.com
This website run by two enthusiastic American travel writers has thousands of pages about all aspects of the city from the practical to essays on cultural matters.

PRIME TRAVEL SITES

www.actv.it
Venice's city transport system runs this informative site where you'll find full route details, timetables and fare structures for the *vaporetto* network.

www.trenitalia.com
The official site of the Italian State Railways with excellent train information and an easy-to-use search facility— good for forward planning.

www.venicebanana.com
Interesting site with good listings, weather, photographs and general information.

www.fodors.com
A travel-planning site where you can research prices and weather, book tickets, cars and rooms, and ask fellow travellers questions; links to other sites.

INTERNET CAFÉ

Ve-Nice Internet Point
✉ Rio Terrà Lista di Spagna 149 (Cannaregio near the station) ☎ 041 275 8217
🕐 Daily 9am–11pm

Getting There

ENTRY REQUIREMENTS AND TRAVEL INSURANCE

For the latest passport and visa information, look up the British embassy website at www.britishembassy.gov.uk or the United States embassy at www.usembassy.gov. EU citizens can obtain health care with the production of the EHIC card. However, insurance to cover illness and theft is strongly advised.

ARRIVING BY CAR

Cars must be left at one of the multistorey car parks at the Tronchetto (linked by boat 2 to the rest of the city) or the more central Piazzale Roma, from where you can walk or catch boats N, 1, 2, 41, 42, 51, 52, 61, DM (Diretto Murano). Rates start at about €26 a day. There are no free car parks and no other parking places; cars parked elsewhere will be towed away and in summer, long lines on the causeway approaching the city are common. Consider leaving your car in Mestre and then taking the train.

AIRPORTS

There are direct flights to Venice from all over the world. Venice has two main airports, Marco Polo and San Giuseppe in Treviso.

60KM (40 MILES)

Treviso Airport ✈
30km (19 miles) to city centre
Bus 1hr, €4.50

✈ **Marco Polo Airport**
8km (5 miles) to city centre
Bus 20 minutes, €3

FROM MARCO POLO

Scheduled internal and international flights (plus a few charters) arrive at Venice's Marco Polo Airport, 8km (5 miles) north of the city hub. For flight information ☎ 041 260 9260; www.veniceairport.it. Connections from Marco Polo to Piazzale Roma take 20–40 minutes and can be made by taxi, blue ATVO Fly/35 bus (041 383 672, www.atvo.it; every 30 minutes 8.10am–11.40pm, 12.20am on Sat; €3 one-way) or less expensive ACTV No. 5 orange city buses (041 272 2111, www.actv.it; 4.08am–1.10am; €2 one-way). Buy tickets for buses before boarding from the office inside the arrivals terminal. Buses leave from the concourse outside the terminal.

BY WATER FROM SAN MARCO

There are two options: a regular boat service, run by Alilaguna, or the more expensive option, the water taxi. To get to the boats take the shuttle bus (navetta), which runs regularly every 5–10 minutes to the lagoon edge. If you want to walk down, it's a 7- to 12-minute walk turning left outside the terminal building. The cheaper option is run by the Società Alilaguna

(☎ 041 240 1701 6555, www. alilaguna.com) with an hourly boat service from Marco Polo to the city. It costs €12 and goes to San Marco, the Lido and Zattere. Make sure you buy your ticket before you leave the airport, the office is close to the arrivals hall exit.

There are four lines: the Linea Alilaguna Rossa, which goes via Murano, the Lido, Arsenale and San Marco to the Zattere; and the Linea Alilaguna Blu, which travels via Murano, the Fondamente Nuove and the Lido to San Zaccaria and San Marco. Choose the service that will take you as near as possible to your hotel; you may find that you will have to connect with an ACTV *vaporetto* for the last stages. The Blu (blue) services start at 6.10am; thereafter the boat leaves at 7.10, then hourly at 10 minutes past the hour until 3.15pm. The Rossa (red) boats start at 9.15am and run hourly until 15 minutes past midnight. Tickets cost €12 and can be bought on board; the journey time is around 75 to 90 minutes. A third line, the Oro (gold) goes directly to San Marco (hourly 8.30–3.30pm). The fourth Aranria (orange) line runs to Murano, Madonna dell' Orto and Guglie at 9.55am then hourly until 3.55pm.

Water taxis are run by the Consorzio Motoscafi Venezia, whose desk is to the left of the exit from the baggage reclaim area in the Marco Polo airport arrivals hall (☎ 041 522 2303, www.motoscafivenezia.it). The taxis run to most points within the city (20 minutes), but the prices are high (officially €45 but buggage surcharges can easily double this).

FROM TREVISO
Treviso airport (☎ 0422 315 111 or 0422 315 1312 ; www.trevisoairport.it), 30km (19 miles) outside the city, is served by low-cost airlines; a ATVO/Eurobus shuttle (☎ 041 383 672; www.atvo.it; €5 each way) connects with some of these. Buy tickets at the ATVO ticket office or foreign exchange outlet.

Trains to Venice arrive at the Venezia Santa Lucia station, often abbreviated as Venezia SL (☎ 041 785870 or 1478 88088, www.trenitalia.it). The station is at the head of the Grand Canal, five minutes' walk from Piazzale Roma; from the quays outside there are frequent *vaporetto* (1, 2 and others) and *motoscafo* (52) boat services to the rest of the city. Be sure the boat you board is heading in the right direction. Many through trains stop on the mainland at Mestre station (☎ 041 929 472), confusingly called Venezia Mestre (Venezia M), without continuing to Venice proper. Check your train is destined for Santa Lucia; if not, catch one of the frequent connecting services at Mestre for the 15-minute trip across the causeway.

GETTING TO YOUR HOTEL

Before you leave, ask your hotel to send you details of how to reach them. You need to know the nearest *vaporetto* stop, the name of the street as well as the *numero civico* (the number given after the district in the address), and the nearest landmark, such as a *campo*, church or museum.

Getting Around

HANDY HINT

Two special tickets are available on ACTV boats: the *Biglietto 24 Ore* (or *Biglietto Giornaliero*), valid for 24 hours (€15); and the *Biglietto 72 Ore*, valid for three days (€30).

VISITORS WITH DISABILITIES

Venice is difficult for visitors with disabilities. Streets are narrow, there are numerous bridges and moving on and off boats is almost impossible. Hotels, galleries and other public spaces are often in historic buildings where conservation restrictions limit access. This said, matters are improving, and the Venetian and Italian state tourist offices can provide lists of appropriate hotels and contact details of Italian associations for those with disabilities.

GONDOLAS

Hiring a gondola is enchanting, but expensive (starting at around €80 for 40 minutes). Bear in mind rates are negotiable, so confirm the rate and duration before departure. Do not be afraid to walk away or haggle if the prices seem too high and there are plenty of gondoliers. If cost is an issue take the cheap public gondalas, the *traghetti*.

The best way to move around Venice is on foot; this is how the Venetians themselves get from place to place, combining walking with the judicious use of public transport in the shape of *vaporetti* (water buses) and *traghetti* (cross-Grand Canal ferries).

BOATS
● ACTV runs two basic types of boat: the general-purpose *vaporetto* and the faster *motoscafi*. Both follow set routes and are numbered at the front of the boat. As the same number boat may run in two directions it is vital at the quays—which usually have separate boarding points for each direction—to make sure you board a boat heading the right way. This is particularly true at the Ferrovia and San Zaccaria, both busy termini for several routes.
● The web of boat routes around Venice is not as confusing as it first seems. The basic route is Line 1 along the Grand Canal (Piazzale Roma–Vallaresso–Lido and back). Line 2 also follows the Grand Canal, but has fewer stops. A second 2 boat runs from San Zaccaria to Piazzale Roma by way of the Giudecca. The other boat you may use is the Laguna Nord (LN), which runs to the islands of Murano and Burano from the Fondamente Nuove. The 'T' shuttle connects Burano and Torcello. The ferry information throughout this guide gives the nearest stop as well as the line number.
● Tickets can be bought at most landing stages, on board boats (with a surcharge), and at shops or tobacconists with an ACTV sticker. One-way tickets (€6, valid for 60 minutes) are valid along the length of the route so the price is the same for one stop or 10 stops. Tickets must be validated in machines at each landing stage before boarding. There are spot fines for riding without a ticket.
● Special tickets are available (▷ panel).
● ACTV runs a less frequent service with a reduced number of stops throughout the night on key Grand Canal routes (indicated by 'N' throughout the guide). Exact times are posted

on the timetables at every quay. Tickets can be bought on board.

TAXIS
● For rides to and from the mainland there are taxi stands at Piazzale Roma ☎ 041 595 2080; Marco Polo Airport ☎ 041 541 6363; and the rail station at Mestre ☎ 041 936 222. Otherwise, call Radio Taxi ☎ 041 595 2080.

TRAGHETTI
● As there are only three main bridges across the Grand Canal, Venice's *traghetti* (ferries) provide an invaluable service. Think of them as bridges and it becomes clear they will save both time and unnecessary mileage. They exist primarily for the convenience of locals, but once you are familiar with the system, judicious use of the *traghetti* will help you get quickly from point to point. Using old gondolas, they ply back and forth at seven strategic points. Quays are usually obscure, so look for the little yellow 'Traghetto' signs. Crossings cost around €0.50, which you hand to the ferryman as you board. Venetians usually stand, but nobody minds if you sit unless the boat is crowded. Be careful with small children, and watch your balance when the boat pushes off.

WATER TAXIS
● Venice's water taxis (*motoscafi*) are fast but extremely expensive (▷ 116–117). The basic rate is €8.70 when the clock starts, and €1.30 per minute after that. Surcharges are levied for each piece of luggage for trips on public holidays and between 10pm and 7am, and for each additional passenger over a maximum of four. You can hail a taxi on a canal, but it is usually easier to call by phone—which means about €6 on the clock before you start ☎ 041 723112 (San Polo) ☎ 041 522 2303 (San Marco) ☎ 041 715787 (Cannaregio) ☎ 041 966170 (airport) ☎ 041 718235 (Santa Lucia rail station).

TOURIST INFORMATION

● Main tourist offices www.turismovenezia.it
✚ H7 ✉ Venice Pavilion, Palazzina del Santi by the Giardinetti Reali ☎ 041 529 8711 ⏰ Daily 10–6
✚ H6 ✉ Piazza San Marco 71/f (Ascensione) ☎ 041 520 8740 ⏰ Daily 9–3.30
● Train station ✚ D4 ☎ 041 529 8727 ⏰ Daily 8–6.30
● Marco Polo Airport office ☎ 041 541 5887 ⏰ Daily 9.30–7.30
● Lido office ✉ Gran Viale Santa Maria Elisabetta 6 ☎ 041 526 5721 ⏰ Summer only 9.30–12.30, 3.30–6
● Piazzale Roma office ✚ D5 ✉ Garage ☎ 041 529 8746 ⏰ Daily 9.30–6.30

LOST PROPERTY

● City streets ☎ 041 522 4576 or visit Vigili Urbani office in Pizzale Roma
● Buses or boats ☎ 041 272 2179 ⏰ Mon–Sat 8–6/4.30 in winter
● Train or station ☎ 041 785 531
● Report lost passports to the police and your consulate
● Report general losses to the main police station ✉ Fondamenta di San Lorenzo, Castello 5053 ☎ 041 270 5511

Essential Facts

MONEY FACTS

Foreign-exchange facilities are available at banks and kiosks throughout the city. Major credit cards are widely accepted in Venice and can be used in ATMs displaying the appropriate sign.

MONEY

The euro is the official currency of Italy. Bank notes in denominations of 5, 10, 20, 50, 100, 200 and 500 euros, and coins in denominations of 1, 2, 5, 10, 20 and 50 cents and 1 and 2 euros were introduced on 1 January 2002.

10 euros

50 euros

200 euros

500 euros

ELECTRICITY
● Current is 220 volts AC (50 cycles), but is suitable for 240-volt appliances.
● Plugs are the Continental two-round-pin.

EMBASSIES & CONSULATES
● France ✉ (Honorary Consul), Palazzo Morosini, Calle del Pestina, Castello 6140 ☎ 041 522 4319
● Netherlands ✉ San Vidal, San Marco 2888 ☎ 041 528 3416
● Republic of Ireland ✉ Piazza Campitelli 3, Rome ☎ 06 697 9121
● UK ✉ Piazzale Donatori di Sangue 2–5, Mestre ☎ 041 505 5990
● USA ✉ Via Principe Amedeo 2/10, 20121 Milan ☎ 02 290351

EMERGENCY PHONE NUMBERS
● Emergency services (police, fire and ambulance) ☎ 113
● Police (Carabinieri) ☎ 112
● Questura (Venice Police Station) ☎ 041 270 5511
● Fire (Vigili di Fuoco) ☎ 113 or 115
● Ambulance ☎ 041 523 0000 or 118
● Hospital and first aid (Ospedale Civile) ✉ Campo SS Giovani e Paolo ☎ 041 529 4111

NATIONAL HOLIDAYS
● 1 Jan: New Year's Day; 6 Jan: Epiphany; Easter Monday; 25 Apr: Liberation Day; 1 May: Labour Day; 2 Jun: Republic Day 15 Aug: Assumption; 1 Nov: All Saints' Day; 8 Dec: Immaculate Conception; 25 Dec: Christmas Day; 26 Dec: Santo Stefano

OPENING HOURS
● Banks: Mon–Fri 8–1.30 (larger branches also 3–4 and resricted Sat opening).
● Churches: Non fixed hours but generally Mon–Sat 9–12, 3–6, Sun 1–5; except St. Mark's and those in the Chorus (▷ 4) scheme.
● Shops: Generally 9–1, 4–8 or 9.30/10–7.30/8; most food shops close Wed

afternoons except in summer, while other shops close Mon mornings except in summer.

POST OFFICES
● Venice's central post office (*posta* or *ufficio postale*) is near the Rialto bridge ➕ H5 ✉ Palazzo delle Poste, Fondaco dei Tedeschi, San Marco 5554 ☎ 041 271 7111 or 041 271 7322; www.poste.it ⏰ Mon–Sat 8.30–6.30
● Stamps (*francobolli*) are available from post offices and *tabacchi* displaying a large 'T' sign.
● Mailboxes are red or blue and are marked *Poste* or *Lettere*. Blue boxes are for faster and more expensive *posta prioritaria* services only.

SENSIBLE PRECAUTIONS
● Venice's tourists are a target for theft, but with a few precautions you can stay safe. Report thefts to your hotel and then to the main police station. Report lost passports to the police or embassy.

TELEPHONES
● Telecom Italia (TI) provides public telephones in bars, on the streets and in TI offices. All are indicated by red or yellow signs showing a telephone dial and receiver. Venice has TI booths in Piazzale Roma ➕ C5 ⏰ 8am–9.30pm; and the main post office.
● Public phones accept coins and most accept phone cards (*schede telefoniche*), available from tobacco shops, TI offices, automatic dispensers or stores displaying a TI sticker.
● The area code for Venice is 041 and must be used when calling from outside and within Venice (numbers in this book include the code).

TOILETS
● Venice has public toilets at the rail station and in larger museums. There are public toilets throughout the city marked with blue and green signs. Most cost €1 and some have attendants to give change if needed.
● In bars and cafés ask for *il gabinetto* or *il bagno*. Do not confuse *signori* (men) with *signore* (women).

HEALTH
Likely hazards include too much sun, air pollution and biting insects.

Water is safe to drink unless marked *acqua non potabile*.

Pharmacies (*una farmacia*) are identified by a green cross and have the same opening hours as shops, but open late on some days as displayed on pharmacy doors. Staff can give advice on minor ailments and dispense many medicines over the counter, including some only available by prescription in other countries.

Remember to bring any prescriptions that might be required to obtain medicine. If you wish to see a doctor (*un medico*), ask at your hotel. For first aid (*pronto soccorso*) or hospital treatment, visit the Ospedale Civile ➕ J4 ✉ Campo Santi Giovanni e Paolo, Castello ☎ 041 529 4111.

ETIQUETTE
● In churches do not wear shorts or miniskirts and cover your arms.
● Do not intrude while church services are in progress.
● Do not eat or drink in churches. Many churches and galleries forbid flash photography, or ban photography altogether.

121

Language

All Italian words are pronounced as written, with each vowel and consonant sounded. Only the letter *h* is silent, but it modifies the sound of other letters. The letter *c* is hard, as in English 'cat', except when followed by *i* or *e*, when it becomes the soft *ch* of 'cello'. Similarly, *g* is soft (as in the English 'giant') when followed by *i* or *e*—*giardino*, *gelati*; otherwise hard (as in 'gas')—*gatto*. Words ending in *o* are almost always masculine in gender (plural: -*i*); those ending in *a* are generally feminine (plural: -*e*). Use the polite second person (*lei*) to speak to strangers and the informal second person (*tu*) to friends or children.

USEFUL WORDS

yes	*sì*
no	*no*
please	*per favore*
thank you	*grazie*
you're welcome	*prego*
excuse me!	*scusi*
where	*dove*
here	*qui*
there	*là*
when	*quando*
now	*adesso*
later	*più tardi*
why	*perchè*
who	*chi*
may I/can I	*posso*
good morning	*buon giorno*
good afternoon/good evening	*buona sera*
good night	*buona notte*
hello/good-bye (informal)	*ciao*
hello (on the telephone)	*pronto*
I'm sorry	*mi dispiace*
left/right	*sinistra/destra*
open/closed	*aperto/chiuso*
good/bad	*buono/cattivo*
big/small	*grande/piccolo*
with/without	*con/senza*
more/less	*più/meno*
hot/cold	*caldo/freddo*
early/late	*presto/ritardo*
today/tomorrow	*oggi/domani*
when?/do you have?	*quando?/avete?*

NUMBERS

1	*uno, una*
2	*due*
3	*tre*
4	*quattro*
5	*cinque*
6	*sei*
7	*sette*
8	*otto*
9	*nove*
10	*dieci*
20	*venti*
30	*trenta*
40	*quaranta*
50	*cinquanta*
100	*cento*
1,000	*mille*

EMERGENCIES

help!	aiuto!
stop, thief!	al ladro!
can you help me, please?	può aiutarmi, per favore?
call the police/an ambulance	chiami la polizia/ un'ambulanza
I have lost my wallet/ passport	ho perso il portafoglio/il pas- saporto
where is the police station?	dov'è il commissari- ato?
where is the hospital?	dov'è l'ospedale?
I don't feel well	non mi sento bene
first aid	pronto soc corso

COLOURS

black	nero
brown	marrone
pink	rosa
red	rosso
orange	arancia
yellow	giallo
green	verde
light blue	celeste
sky blue	azzuro
purple	viola
white	bianco
grey	grigio

USEFUL PHRASES

how are you? (informal)	come sta/stai?
I'm fine	sto bene
I do not understand	non ho capito
how much is it?	quant'è?
do you have a room?	avete camere libere?
how much per night?	quanto costa una notte?
with bath/shower	con vasca/doccia
when is breakfast served?	a che ora è servita la colazione?
where is the train/bus station?	dov'è la stazione ferroviaria degli autobus
where are we?	dove siamo?
do I have to get off here?	devo scendere qui?
I'm looking for ...	cerco ...
where can I buy ...?	dove posso comprare ...?
a table for ... please	un tavolo per ... per favore
The bill, please	il conto, per favore
we didn't have this	non abbiamo avuto questo
where are the toilets?	dove sono i gabinetti?

DAYS/MONTHS

Monday	lunedì
Tuesday	martedì
Wednesday	mercoledì
Thursday	giovedì
Friday	venerdì
Saturday	sabato
Sunday	Domenica
January	gennaio
February	febbraio
March	marzo
April	aprile
May	maggio
June	giugno
July	luglio
August	agosto
September	settembre
October	ottobre
November	novembre
December	dicembre

Timeline

MARCO POLO

Born in Venice in 1254, Marco Polo left with his father in 1269 on a journey that would last two decades. In 1275 he arrived in the court of Kublai Khan, where he served the Mongol emperor until 1295. In 1298 he was captured by the Genoese. It was from prison that he dictated his *Description of the World*.

ANTONIO VIVALDI

Vivaldi was born in Venice in 1678. Although ordained as a priest, he devoted his life to music, teaching violin at La Pietà orphanage, whose girls received music training as part of their state-funded education. La Pietà's orchestra enabled Vivaldi to create a wealth of musical compositions, including his most famous work the 'Four Seasons'.

$800BC$ Sporadic settlement of the lagoon by the Venetii and Euganei tribes.

$250BC$ Rome conquers Venetia and founds important colonies at Padua, Verona, Altinium and Aquileia.

$AD402$ Alaric the Goth sacks Altinium and other northeastern colonies. A vision of the Virgin guides refugees to an island in the lagoon.

421 According to legend Venice is founded on 25 March, the Feast Day of the Virgin Mary.

453 Aquileia is sacked by Attila the Hun, prompting another exodus of refugees to the lagoon.

697 The first Doge (leader) of Venice, Paoluccio Anafesto, is elected.

810 Lagoon dwellers gather on the more easily defended islands of the Rialto.

828 Venetian merchants steal the relics of St. Mark from Alexandria.

1171 Venice's six districts are founded.

1204 Venice sacks Constantinople and acquires much of the former Byzantine Empire.

1380 Victory over the Genoese at the Battle of Chioggia. Venice wins naval supremacy in the Adriatic and Mediterranean.

1406 Venice defeats Padua and Verona to lay the foundations of a mainland empire.

1453 Venice's power is at its height, but the Turks take Constantinople. Over the next 200 years they will also take the islands of Cyprus and Crete.

1498 Vasco da Gama's discovery of the Cape route to the East weakens Venice's trading monopolies.

1718 The loss of Morea marks the end of Venice's maritime empire.

1797 Napolean invades Italy: the last doge abdicates and the Venetian Republic comes to an end.

1814 After Napolean's defeat, the Congress of Vienna cedes Venice and the Veneto to Austria.

1866 Venice joins a united Italy.

1966 Devastating floods ravage Venice in November. Over 5,000 Venetians lose their homes and many works of arts are destroyed.

1988 Work on the MOSE flood barrier begins; after delays, the project is reapproved in 2003.

2007 Work on the MOSE project is back on course after budgetary problems in 2006.

COURTESAN AND VENETIAN GREED

At the end of the 16th century, the city contained 11,654 women of the night. This compared with 2,889 patrician women; 1,936 burghers; and 2,508 nuns. Taxes from prostitution funded an estimated 12 galleys (ships). In the 18th century, according to one contemporary report, 'Venetians did not taste their pleasures, but swallowed them whole'. Another observer reported that 'the men are women, the women are men, and all are monkeys'.

From the left: Marco Polo; The Lion of St. Mark; a Venetian doge; puppet in the Ca' Goldini; statue of Goldini in Campo San Bartolomeo; sea picture depicting the doge setting out in the Bucentaur; avoiding the floods

Index

Venice's
25 Best

WRITTEN BY Tim Jepson
UPDATED BY Mike Gerrard
DESIGN WORK Jacqueline Bailey
COVER DESIGN Tigist Getachew
INDEXER Marie Lorimer
IMAGE RETOUCHING AND REPRO Michael Moody and Sarah Montgomery
EDITORIAL MANAGEMENT Apostrophe S Limited
REVIEWING EDITOR Linda Cabasin
SERIES EDITOR Marie-Claire Jefferies

© AA Media Limited 2009 (registered office: Fanum House, Basing View, Basingstoke, Hampshire RG21 4EA, registered number 06112600).

All rights reserved. Published in the United States by Fodor's Travel, a division of Random House, Inc., and simultaneously in Canada by Random House of Canada Limited, Toronto. Distributed by Random House, Inc., New York. No maps, illustrations, or other portions of this book may be reproduced in any form without written permission from the publishers.

Fodor's is a registered trademark of Random House, Inc.
Published in the United Kingdom by AA Publishing

ISBN 978-1-4000-0385-3

SEVENTH EDITION

IMPORTANT TIP
Time inevitably brings changes, so always confirm prices, travel facts, and other perishable information when it matters. Although Fodor's cannot accept responsibility for errors, you can use this guide in the confidence that we have taken every care to ensure its accuracy.

SPECIAL SALES
This book is available for special discounts for bulk purchases for sales promotions or premiums. Special editions, including personalized covers, excerpts of existing books, and corporate imprints, can be created in large quantities for special needs. For more information, write to Special Markets/Premium Sales, 1745 Broadway, MD 6–2, New York, NY 10019 or email specialmarkets@randomhouse.com.

Color separation by Keenes, Andover, UK
Printed and bound by Leo Paper Products, China
10 9 8 7 6 5 4 3 2

A04461
Maps in this title produced from map data © New Holland Publishing (South Africa) (Pty) Ltd, 2006
Transport map © Communicarta Ltd, UK

The Automobile Association wishes to thank the following photographers, companies and picture libraries for their assistance in the preparation of this book.

Abbreviations for the picture credits are as follows – (t) top; (b) bottom; (l) left; (r) right; (c) center; (AA) AA World Travel Library.

1 AA/A Mockford & N Bonetti; 2 AA/S McBride; 3 AA/S McBride; 4t AA/S McBride; 4c AA/D Miterdiri; 5t AA/S McBride; 5b AA/A Mockford & N Bonetti; 6t AA/S McBride; 6cl AA/A Mockford & N Bonetti; 6c AA/S McBride; 6cr AA/A Mockford & N Bonetti; 6bl AA/D Miterdiri; 6bc AA/A Mockford & N Bonetti; 6br AA/A Mockford & N Bonetti; 7t AA/S McBride; 7cl AA/S McBride; 7c AA/A Mockford & N Bonetti; 7cr AA/A Mockford & N Bonetti; 7bl AA/A Mockford & N Bonetti; 7bc AA/A Mockford & N Bonetti; 7br AA/S McBride; 8 AA/S McBride; 9 AA/S McBride; 10t AA/S McBride; 10cr AA/C Sawyer; 10c AA/C Sawyer; 10/11cb AA/A Mockford & N Bonetti; 10/11b AA/D Miterdiri; 11t AA/S McBride; 11ct AA/A Mockford & N Bonetti; 11c AA/S McBride; 12 AA/D Miterdiri; 13t AA/S McBride; 13ct AA/A Mockford & N Bonetti 13c Photodisc; 13cb AA/A Mockford & N Bonetti; 13b AA/A Mockford & N Bonetti; 14t AA/S McBride; 14ct AA/A Mockford & N Bonetti; 14c AA/A Mockford & N Bonetti; 14cb AA/A Mockford & N Bonetti; 14b AA/A Mockford & N Bonetti; 15 A Mockford & N Bonetti; 16t AA/S McBride; 16ct AA/A Mockford & N Bonetti; 16c AA/A Mockford & N Bonetti; 16cb AA/A Mockford & N Bonetti; 16b AA/A Mockford & N Bonetti; 17t AA/S McBride; 17ct AA/D Miterdiri; 17c AA/A Mockford & N Bonetti; 17cb AA/A Mockford & N Bonetti; 17b AA/A Mockford & N Bonetti 18t AA/S McBride; 18ct AA/S McBride; 18c AA/A Mockford & N Bonetti; 18cb AA/J Wyand; 18b AA/A Mockford & N Bonetti; 19t AA/A Mockford & N Bonetti; 19ct AA/S McBride; 19c AA/A Mockford & N Bonetti; 19cb AA/A Mockford & N Bonetti; 19b AA/A Mockford & N Bonetti; 20/21 AA/A Mockford & N Bonetti; 24l AA/C Sawyer; 24tr AA/C Sawyer; 24cr AA/A Mockford & N Bonetti; 25t AA/A Mockford & N Bonetti; 25cl AA/A Mockford & N Bonetti; 25cr AA/C Sawyer; 26 AA/D Miterdiri; 26/27 AA/C Sawyer; 28l AA/A Mockford & N Bonetti; 28tr AA/A Mockford & N Bonetti; 28/29 AA/S McBride; 29t AA/C Sawyer; 29bl AA/C Sawyer; 29br AA/A Mockford & N Bonetti; 30l AA/A Mockford & N Bonetti; 30tr AA/C Saywer; 30cr AA/D Miterdiri; 31tl AA/A Mockford & N Bonetti; 31bl AA/A Mockford & N Bonetti; 31r AA/S McBride; 32l AA/A Mockford & N Bonetti; 32c AA/A Mockford & N Bonetti; 32r AA/A Mockford & N Bonetti; 33l AA/A Mockford & N Bonetti; 33r AA/A Mockford & N Bonetti; 34t AA/A Mockford & N Bonetti; 34bl AA/A Mockford & N Bonetti; 34br AA/C Saywer; 35t AA/A Mockford & N Bonetti; 35bl AA/A Mockford & N Bonetti; 35br AA/A Mockford & N Bonetti; 36 AA/A Mockford & N Bonetti; 37 AA/A Mockford & N Bonetti; 38 Photodisc; 39 AA/M Chaplow; 40 Brand X Pictures; 41 AA/A Kouprianoff; 42 AA/C Sawyer; 43 AA/A Mockford & N Bonetti; 47t AA/A Mockford & N Bonetti; 47r AA/C Sawyer; 48l AA/S McBride; 48c AA/S McBride; 48r AA/D Miterdiri; 49l AA/A Mockford & N Bonetti; 49c AA/A Mockford & N Bonetti; 49r AA/A Mockford & N Bonetti; 50l AA/D Miterdiri; 50/51 AA/C Sawyer; 50cr AA/C Sawyer; 51cl AA/D Miterdiri; 51r AA/A Mockford & N Bonetti; 52l AA/A Mockford & N Bonetti; 52c AA/A Mockford & N Bonetti; 52r AA/A Mockford & N Bonetti; 53l AA/S McBride; 53r AA/S McBride; 54l AA/A Mockford & N Bonetti; 54/55 AA/A Mockford & N Bonetti; 54cr AA/A Mockford & N Bonetti; 55cl AA/A Mockford & N Bonetti; 55r AA/A Mockford & N Bonetti; 56t AA/A Mockford & N Bonetti; 56bl AA/C Sawyer; 56br AA/A Mockford & N Bonetti; 57t AA/A Mockford & N Bonetti; 57bl AA/C Sawyer; 57br AA/A Mockford & N Bonetti; 58 AA/A Mockford & N Bonetti; 59 AA/C Sawyer; 60 AA/A Mockford & N Bonetti; 61 Digital Vision; 62 Photodisc; 63 AA/T Harris; 64 AA/E Meacher; 65 AA/A Mockford & N Bonetti; 68t AA/A Mockford & N Bonetti; 68cl AA/S McBride; 68/69 AA/A Mockford & N Bonetti; 69t AA/A Mockford & N Bonetti; 69cl AA/S McBride; 69cr AA/A Mockford & N Bonetti; 70l AA/C Sawyer; 70tr AA/S McBride; 70/71 AA/C Sawyer; 71t AA/S McBride; 71b AA/C Sawyer; 72t AA/D Miterdiri; 72cl AA/A Mockford & N Bonetti; 72cr AA/S McBride; 73t AA/A Mockford & N Bonetti; 72/73 AA/C Sawyer; 73cr AA/C Sawyer; 74t AA/A Mockford & N Bonetti; 74bl AA/C Sawyer; 74br AA/C Sawyer; 75t AA/A Mockford & N Bonetti; 75b AA/A Mockford & N Bonetti; 76 AA/S McBride; 77 AA/A Mockford & N Bonetti; 78 Brand X Pictures; 79 AA/C Sawyer; 80 AA/C Sawyer; 81 AA/A Mockford & N Bonetti; 84l AA/C Sawyer; 84r AA/A Mockford & N Bonetti; 85l AA/S McBride; 85r AA/S McBride; 86l AA/A Mockford & N Bonetti; 86tr AA/A Mockford & N Bonetti; 86/87 AA/A Mockford & N Bonetti; 87t AA/A Mockford & N Bonetti; 87cl AA/A Mockford & N Bonetti; 87cr AA/A Mockford & N Bonetti; 88l AA/A Mockford & N Bonetti; 88c AA/A Mockford & N Bonetti; 88r AA/A Mockford & N Bonetti; 89l AA/A Mockford & N Bonetti; 89c AA/A Mockford & N Bonetti; 89r AA/A Mockford & N Bonetti; 90l AA/A Mockford & N Bonetti; 90r AA/A Mockford & N Bonetti; 91t AA/A Mockford & N Bonetti; 91bl AA/A Mockford & N Bonetti; 91br AA/C Sawyer; 92t AA/A Mockford & N Bonetti; 92bl AA/A Mockford & N Bonetti; 92br AA/S McBride; 93 AA/A Mockford & N Bonetti; 94 AA/C Sawyer; 95 AA/A Mockford & N Bonetti; 96 Brand X Pictures; 97 AA/A Mockford & N Bonetti; 100 AA/C Sawyer; 101l AA/S McBride; 101c AA/S McBride; 101r AA/C Sawyer; 102 AA/A Mockford & N Bonetti; 102/103t AA/A Mockford & N Bonetti; 102/103c AA/A Mockford & N Bonetti; 103 AA/A Mockford & N Bonetti; 104l AA/A Mockford & N Bonetti; 104c AA/C Sawyer; 104r AA/A Mockford & N Bonetti; 105 AA/A Mockford & N Bonetti; 106t AA/A Mockford & N Bonetti; 106bl AA/C Sawyer; 106br AA/A Mockford & N Bonetti; 107 AA/A Mockford & N Bonetti; 108t AA/C Sawyer; 108ct Photodisc; 108c AA/C Sawyer; 108cb AA/A Mockford & N Bonetti; 108b AA/D Miterdiri; 109 AA/C Sawyer; 110 AA/C Sawyer; 111 AA/C Sawyer; 112 AA/C Sawyer; 113 AA/A Mockford & N Bonetti; 114 AA/A Mockford & N Bonetti; 115t AA/A Mockford & N Bonetti; 115b AA/A Mockford & N Bonetti; 116 AA/A Mockford & N Bonetti; 117 AA/A Mockford & N Bonetti; 118 AA/A Mockford & N Bonetti; 119 AA/A Mockford & N Bonetti; 120t AA/A Mockford & N Bonetti; 120b European Central Bank; 121 AA/A Mockford & N Bonetti; 122t AA/A Mockford & N Bonetti; 122c AA/A Mockford & N Bonetti; 123t AA/A Mockford & N Bonetti; 123c AA/A Mockford & N Bonetti; 124t AA/A Mockford & N Bonetti; 124bl AA; 124bc AA/A Mockford & N Bonetti; 124br AA; 124/125 AA/A Mockford & N Bonetti; 125t AA/A Mockford & N Bonetti; 125bl AA/A Mockford & N Bonetti; 125bc AA; 125br AA/D Miterdiri

Every effort has been made to trace the copyright holders, and we apologize in advance for any unintentional omissions or errors. We would be pleased to apply any corrections in any following edition of this publication.